Lays of Ancient Rome

CENTURY BOUND

Lays of Ancient Rome

By Thomas Babington Macaulay

Published by Century Bound

First Published
1842

CONTENTS

LAYS OF ANCIENT ROME

That what is called the history of the Kings and early Consuls of Rome is to a great extent fabulous, few scholars have, since the time of Beaufort, ventured to deny. It is certain that, more than three hundred and sixty years after the date ordinarily assigned for the foundation of the city, the public records were, with scarcely an exception, destroyed by the Gauls. It is certain that the oldest annals of the commonwealth were compiled more than a century and a half after this destruction of the records. It is certain, therefore, that the great Latin writers of the Augustan age did not possess those materials, without which a trustworthy account of the infancy of the republic could not possibly be framed. Those writers own, indeed, that the chronicles to which they had access were filled with battles that were never fought, and Consuls that were never inaugurated; and we have abundant proof that, in these chronicles, events of the greatest importance, such as the issue of the war with Porsena and the issue of the war with Brennus, were grossly misrepresented. Under these circumstances a wise man will look with great suspicion on the legend which has come down to us. He will perhaps be inclined to regard the princes who are said to have founded the civil and religious institutions of Rome, the sons of Mars, and the husband of Egeria, as mere mythological personages, of the same class with Perseus and Ixion. As he draws nearer to the confines of authentic history, he will become less and less hard of belief. He will admit that the most important parts of the narrative have some foundation in truth. But he will distrust almost all the details, not only because they seldom rest on any solid evidence, but also because he will constantly detect in them, even when they are within the limits of physical possibility, that peculiar character, more easily understood than defined, which distinguishes the creations of the imagination from the realities of the world in which we live.

The early history of Rome is indeed far more poetical than anything else in Latin literature. The loves of the Vestal and the God of War, the cradle laid among the reeds of Tiber, the fig-tree, the she-wolf, the shepherd's cabin, the recognition, the fratricide, the rape of the Sabines, the death of Tarpeia, the fall of Hostus Hostilius, the struggle of Mettus Curtius through the marsh, the women rushing with torn raiment and dishevelled hair between their fathers and their husbands, the nightly meetings of Numa and the Nymph by the well in the sacred grove, the fight of the three Romans and the three Albans, the purchase of the Sibylline books, the crime of Tullia, the simulated madness of Brutus, the ambiguous reply of the Delphian oracle to the Tarquins, the wrongs of Lucretia, the heroic actions of Horatius Cocles, of Scaevola, and of Cloelia, the battle of Regillus won by the aid of Castor and Pollux, the defense of Cremera, the touching story of Coriolanus, the still more touching story of Virginia, the wild legend about the draining of the Alban lake, the combat between Valerius Corvus and the gigantic Gaul, are among the many instances which will at once suggest themselves to every reader.

In the narrative of Livy, who was a man of fine imagination, these stories retain much of their genuine character. Nor could even the tasteless Dionysius distort and mutilate them into mere prose. The poetry shines, in spite of him, through the dreary pedantry of his eleven books. It is discernible in the most tedious and in the most superficial modern works on the early times of Rome. It enlivens the dulness of the Universal History, and gives a charm to the most meagre abridgements of Goldsmith.

Even in the age of Plutarch there were discerning men who rejected the popular account of the foundation of Rome, because that account appeared to them to have the air, not of a history, but of a romance or a drama. Plutarch, who was displeased at their incredulity, had nothing better to say in reply to their arguments than that chance sometimes turns poet, and produces trains of events not to be distinguished from the most elaborate plots which are constructed by art. But though the existence of a poetical element in the early history of the Great City was detected so many ages ago, the first critic who distinctly saw from what source that poetical element had been derived was James Perizonius, one of the most acute and learned antiquaries of the seventeenth century. His theory, which in his own days attracted little or no notice, was revived in the present generation by Niebuhr, a man who would have been the first writer of his time, if his talent for communicating truths had borne any proportion to his talent for investigating them. That theory has been adopted by several eminent scholars of our own country, particularly by the Bishop of St. David's, by Professor Malde, and by the lamented Arnold. It appears to be now generally received by men conversant with classical antiquity; and indeed it rests on such strong proofs, both internal and external, that it will not be easily subverted

A popular exposition of this theory, and of the evidence by which it is supported, may not be without interest even for readers who are unacquainted with the ancient languages.

The Latin literature which has come down to us is of later date than the commencement of the Second Punic War, and consists almost exclusively of works fashioned on Greek models. The Latin metres, heroic, elegiac, lyric, and dramatic, are of Greek origin. The best Latin epic poetry is the feeble echo of the Iliad and Odyssey. The best Latin eclogues are imitations of Theocritus. The plan of the most finished didactic poem in the Latin tongue was taken from Hesiod. The Latin tragedies are bad copies of the masterpieces of Sophocles and Euripides. The Latin philosophy was borrowed, without alteration, from the Portico and the Academy; and the great Latin orators constantly proposed to themselves as patterns the speeches of Demosthenes and Lysias.

But there was an earlier Latin literature, a literature truly Latin, which has wholly perished, which had, indeed almost wholly perished long before those whom we are in the habit of regarding as the greatest Latin writers were born. That literature abounded with metrical romances, such as are found in every country where there is much curiosity and intelligence, but little reading and writing. All human beings, not utterly savage, long for some information about past times, and are delighted by narratives which present pictures to the eye of the mind. But it is only in very enlightened communities that books are readily accessible. Metrical composition, therefore, which, in a highly civilized nation, is a mere luxury, is, in nations imperfectly civilized, almost a necessary of life, and is valued less on account of the pleasure which it gives to the ear, than on account of the help which it gives to the memory. A man who can invent or embellish an interesting story, and put it into a form which others may easily retain in their recollection, will always be highly esteemed by a people eager for amusement and information, but destitute of libraries. Such is the origin of ballad-poetry, a species of composition which scarcely ever fails to spring up and flourish in every society, at a certain point in the progress towards refinement. Tacitus informs us that songs were the only memorials of the past which the ancient Germans possessed. We learn from Lucan and from Ammianus Marcellinus that the brave actions of the ancient Gauls were commemorated in the verses of Bards. During many ages, and through many revolution, minstrelsy retained its influence over both the Teutonic and the Celtic race. The vengeance exacted by the spouse of Attila for the murder of Siegfried was celebrated in rhymes, of which Germany is still justly proud. The exploits of Athelstane were commemorated by the Anglo-Saxons and those of Canute by the Danes, in rude poems, of which a few fragments have come down to us. The chants of the Welsh harpers preserved, through ages of darkness, a faint and doubtful memory of Arthur. In the Highlands of Scotland may still be gleaned some relics of the old songs about Cuthullin and Fingal. The long struggle of the Servians against the Ottoman power was recorded in lays full of martial spirit. We learn from Herrera that, when a Peruvian Inca died, men of skill were appointed to celebrate him in verses, which all the people learned by heart, and sang in public on days of festival. The feats of Kurroglou, the great freebooter of Turkistan, recounted in ballads composed by himself, are known in every village of northern Persia. Captain Beechey heard the bards of the Sandwich Islands recite the heroic achievements of Tamehameha, the most illustrious of their kings. Mungo Park found in the heart of Africa a class of singing men, the only annalists of their rude tribes, and heard them tell the story of the victory which Damel, the negro prince of the Jaloffs, won over Abdulkader, the Mussulman tyrant of Foota Torra. This species of poetry attained a high degree of excellence among the Castilians, before they began to copy Tuscan patterns. It attained a still higher degree of excellence among the English and the Lowland Scotch, during the fourteenth, fifteenth, and sixteenth centuries. But it reached its full perfection in ancient Greece; for there can be no doubt that the great Homeric poems are generically ballads, though widely distinguished from all other ballads, and indeed from almost all other human composition, by transcendent sublimity and beauty.

As it is agreeable to general experience that, at a certain stage in the progress of society, ballad-poetry should flourish, so is it also agreeable to general experience that, at a subsequent stage in the progress of society, ballad-poetry should be undervalued and neglected. Knowledge advances; manners change; great foreign models of composition are studied and imitated. The phraseology of the old minstrels becomes obsolete. Their versification, which, having received its laws only from the ear, abounds in irregularities, seems licentious and uncouth. Their simplicity appears beggarly when compared with the quaint forms and gaudy coloring of such artists as Cowley and Gongora. The ancient lays, unjustly despised by the learned and polite, linger for a time in the memory of the vulgar, and are at length too often irretrievably lost. We cannot wonder that the ballads of Rome should have altogether disappeared, when we remember how very narrowly, in spite of the invention of printing, those of our own country and those of Spain escaped the same fate. There is indeed little doubt that oblivion covers many English songs equal to any that were published by Bishop Percy, and many Spanish songs as good as the best of those which have been so happily translated by Mr. Lockhart. Eighty years ago England possessed only one tattered copy of Childe Waters and Sir Cauline, and Spain only one tattered copy of the noble poem of the Cid. The snuff of a candle, or a mischievous dog, might in a moment have deprived the world forever of any of those fine compositions. Sir Walter Scott, who united to the fire of a great poet the minute curiosity and patient diligence of a great antiquary, was but just in time to save the precious relics of the Minstrelsy of the Border. In Germany, the lay of the Nibelungs had been long utterly forgotten, when, in the eighteenth century, it was, for the first time, printed from a manuscript in the old library of a noble family. In truth, the only people who, through their whole passage from simplicity to the highest civilization, never for a moment ceased to love and admire their old ballads, were the Greeks.

That the early Romans should have had ballad-poetry, and that this poetry should have perished, is therefore not strange. It would, on the contrary, have been strange if these things had not come to pass; and we should be justified in pronouncing them highly probable even if we had no direct evidence on the subject. But we have direct evidence of unquestionable authority.

Ennius, who flourished in the time of the Second Punic War, was regarded in the Augustan age as the father of Latin poetry. He was, in truth, the father of the second school of Latin poetry, the only school of which the works have descended to us. But from Ennius himself we learn that there were poets who stood to him in the same relation in which the author of the romance of Count Alarcos stood to Garcilaso, or the author of the Lytell Geste of Robyn Hode to Lord Surrey. Ennius speaks of verses which the Fauns and the Bards were wont to chant in the old time, when none had yet studied the graces of speech, when none had yet climbed the peaks sacred to the Goddesses of Grecian song. "Where," Cicero mournfully asks, "are those old verses now?"

Contemporary with Ennius was Quintus Fabius Pactor, the earliest of the Roman annalists. His account of the infancy and youth of Romulus and Remus has been preserved by Dionysius, and contains a very remarkable reference to the ancient Latin poetry. Fabius says that, in his time, his countrymen were still in the habit of singing ballads about the Twins. "Even in the hut of Faustulus,"— so these old lays appear to have run,— "the children of Rhea and Mars were, in port and in spirit, not like unto swineherds or cowherds, but such that men might well guess them to be of the blood of kings and gods."

Cato the Censor, who also lived in the days of he Second Punic War, mentioned this lost literature in his lost work on the antiquities of his country. Many ages, he said, before his time, there were ballads in praise of illustrious men; and these ballads it was the fashion for the guests at banquets to sing in turn while the piper played. "Would," exclaims Cicero, "that we still had the old ballads of which Cato speaks!"

Valerius Maximus gives us exactly similar information, without mentioning his authority, and observes that the ancient Roman ballads were probably of more benefit to the young than all the lectures of the Athenian schools, and that to the influence of the national poetry were to be ascribed the virtues of such men as Camillus and Fabricus.

Varro, whose authority on all questions connected with the antiquities of his country is entitled to the greatest respect, tells us that at banquets it was once the fashion for boys to sing, sometimes with and sometimes without instrumental music, ancient ballads in praise of men of former times. These young performers, he observes, were of unblemished character, a circumstance which he probably mentioned because, among the Greeks, and indeed, in his time among the Romans also, the morals of singing boys were in no high repute.

The testimony of Horace, though given incidentally, confirms the statements of Cato, Valerius Maximus, and Varro. The poet predicts that, under the peaceful administration of Augustus, the Romans will, over their full goblets, sing to the pipe, after the fashion of their fathers, the deeds of brave captains, and the ancient legends touching the origin of the city.

The proposition, then, that Rome had ballad-poetry is not merely in itself highly probable, but is fully proved by direct evidence of the greatest weight.

This proposition being established, it becomes easy to understand why the early history of the city is unlike almost everything else in Latin literature, native where almost everything else is borrowed, imaginative where almost everything else is prosaic. We can scarcely hesitate to pronounce that the magnificent, pathetic, and truly national legends, which present so striking a contrast to all that surrounds them, are broken and defaced fragments of that early poetry which, even in the age of Cato the Censor, had become antiquated, and of which Tully had never heard a line.

That this poetry should have been suffered to perish will not appear strange when we consider how complete was the triumph of the Greek genius over the public mind of Italy. It is probable that, at an early period, Homer and Herodotus furnished some hints to the Latin Minstrels; but it was not till after the war with Pyrrhus that the poetry of Rome began to put off its old Ausonian character. The transformation was soon consummated. The conquered, says Horace, led captive the conquerors. It was precisely at the time at which the Roman people rose to unrivalled political ascendency that they stooped to pass under the intellectual yoke. It was precisely at the time at which the sceptre departed from Greece that the empire of her language and of her arts became universal and despotic. The revolution indeed was not effected without a struggle. Naevius seems to have been the last of the ancient line of poets. Ennius was the founder of a new dynasty. Naevius celebrated the First Punic War in Saturnian verse, the old national verse of Italy. Ennius sang the Second Punic War in numbers borrowed from the Iliad. The elder poet, in the epitaph which he wrote for himself, and which is a fine specimen of the early Roman diction and versification, plaintively boasted that the Latin language had died with him. Thus what to Horace appeared to be the first faint dawn of Roman literature appeared to Naevius to be its hopeless setting. In truth, one literature was setting, and another dawning.

The victory of the foreign taste was decisive; and indeed we can hardly blame the Romans for turning away with contempt from the rude lays which had delighted their fathers, and giving their whole admiration to the immortal productions of Greece. The national romances, neglected by the great and the refined whose education had been finished at Rhodes or Athens, continued, it may be supposed, during some generations to delight the vulgar. While Virgil, in hexameters of exquisite modulation, described the sports of rustics, those rustics were still singing their wild Saturnian ballads. It is not improbable that, at the time when Cicero lamented the irreparable loss of the poems mentioned by Cato, a search among the nooks of the Appenines, as active as the search which Sir Walter Scott made among the descendents of the mosstroopers of Liddesdale, might have brought to light many fine remains of ancient minstrelsy. No such search was made. The Latin ballads perished forever. Yet discerning critics have thought that they could still perceive in the early history of Rome numerous fragments of this lost poetry, as the traveller on classic ground sometimes finds, built into the heavy wall of a fort or convent, a pillar rich with acanthus leaves, or a frieze where the Amazons and Bacchanals seem to live. The theatres and temples of the Greek and the Roman were degraded into the quarries of the Turk and the Goth. Even so did the ancient Saturnian poetry become the quarry in which a crowd of orators and annalists found the materials for their prose.

It is not difficult to trace the process by which the old songs were transmuted into the form which they now wear. Funeral panegyric and chronicle appear to have been the intermediate links which connected the lost ballads with the histories now extant. From a very early period it was the usage that an oration should be pronounced over the remains of a noble Roman. The orator, as we learn from Polybius, was expected, on such occasions, to recapitulate all the services which the ancestors of the deceased had, from the earliest time, rendered to the commonwealth. There can be little doubt that the speaker on whom this duty was imposed would make use of all the stories suited to his purpose which were to be found in the popular lays. There can be as little doubt that the family of an eminent man would preserve a copy of the speech which had been pronounced over his corpse. The compilers of the early chronicles would have recourse to these speeches; and the great historians of a later period would have recourse to the chronicles.

It may be worth while to select a particular story, and to trace its probable progress through these stages. The description of the migration of the Fabian house to Cremera is one of the finest of the many fine passages which lie thick in the earlier books of Livy. The Consul, clad in his military garb, stands in the vestibule of his house marshalling his clan, three hundred and six fighting men, all of the same proud patrician blood, all worthy to be attended by the fasces, and to command the legions. A sad and anxious retinue of friends accompanies the adventurers through the streets; but the voice of lamentation is drowned by the shouts of admiring thousands. As the procession passes the Capitol, prayers and vows are poured forth, but in vain. The devoted band, leaving Janus on the right, marches to its doom, through the Gate of Evil Luck. After achieving high deeds of valor against overwhelming numbers, all perish save one child, the stock from which the great Fabian race was destined again to spring, for the safety and glory of the commonwealth. That this fine romance, the details of which are so full of poetical truth, and so utterly destitute of all show of historical truth, came originally from some lay which had often been sung with great applause at banquets is in the highest degree probable. Nor is it difficult to imagine a mode in which the transmission might have taken place. The celebrated Quintus Fabius Maximus, who died about twenty years before the First Punic War, and more than forty years before Ennius was born, is said to have been interred with extraordinary pomp. In the eulogy pronounced over his body all the great exploits of his ancestors were doubtless recounted and exaggerated. If there were then extant songs which gave a vivid and touching description of an event, the saddest and the most glorious in the long history of the Fabian house, nothing could be more natural than that the panegyrist should borrow from such songs their finest touches, in order to adorn his speech. A few generations later the songs would perhaps be forgotten, or remembered only by shepherds and vinedressers. But the speech would certainly be preserved in the archives of the Fabian nobles. Fabius Pictor would be well acquainted with a document so interesting to his personal feelings, and would insert large extracts from it in his rude chronicle. That chronicle, as we know, was the oldest to which Livy had access. Livy would at a glance distinguish the bold strokes of the forgotten poet from the dull and feeble narrative by which they were surrounded, would retouch them with a delicate and powerful pencil, and would make them immortal.

That this might happen at Rome can scarcely be doubted; for something very like this has happened in several countries, and, among others, in our own. Perhaps the theory of Perizonius cannot be better illustrated than by showing that what he supposes to have taken place in ancient times has, beyond all doubt, taken place in modern times.

"History," says Hume with the utmost gravity, "has preserved some instances of Edgar's amours, from which, as from a specimen, we may form a conjecture of the rest." He then tells very agreeably the stories of Elfleda and Elfrida, two stories which have a most suspicious air of romance, ad which, indeed, greatly resemble, in their character, some of the legends of early Rome. He cites, as his authority for these two tales, the chronicle of William of Malmesbury, who lived in the time of King Stephen. The great majority of readers suppose that the device by which Elfleda was substituted for her young mistress, the artifice by which Athelwold obtained the hand of Elfrida, the detection of that artifice, the hunting party, and the vengeance of the amorous king, are things about which there is no more doubt than about the execution of Anne Boleyn, or the slitting of Sir John Coventry's nose. But when we turn to William of Malmesbury, we find that Hume, in his eagerness to relate these pleasant fables, has overlooked one very important circumstance. William does indeed tell both the stories; but he gives us distinct notice that he does not warrant their truth, and that they rest on no better authority than that of ballads.

Such is the way in which these two well-known tales have been handed down. They originally appeared in a poetical form. They found their way from ballads into an old chronicle. The ballads perished; the chronicle remained. A great historian, some centuries after the ballads had been altogether forgotten, consulted the chronicle. He was struck by the lively coloring of these ancient fictions: he transferred them to his pages; and thus we find inserted as unquestionable facts, in a narrative which is likely to last as long as the English tongue, the inventions of some minstrel whose works were probably never committed to writing, whose name is buried in oblivion, and whose dialect has become obsolete. It must, then, be admitted to be possible, or rather highly probable, that the stories of Romulus and Remus, and of the Horatii and Curiatti, may have had a similar origin.

Castilian literature will furnish us with another parallel case. Mariana, the classical historian of Spain, tells the story of the ill-starred marriage which the King Don Alonso brought about between the heirs of Carrion and the two daughters of the Cid. The Cid bestowed a princely dower on the sons-in-law. But the young men were base and proud, cowardly and cruel. They were tried in danger, and found wanting. They fled before the Moors, and once, when a lion broke out of his den, they ran and crouched in an unseemly hiding-place. They knew that they were despised, and took counsel how they might be avenged. They parted from their father-in-law with many signs of love, and set forth on a journey with Doña Elvira and Doña Sol. In a solitary place the bridegrooms seized their brides, stripped them, scourged them, and departed, leaving them for dead. But one of the House of Bivar, suspecting foul play, had followed the travellers in disguise. The ladies were brought back safe to the house of their father. Complaint was made to the king. It was adjudged by the Cortes that the dower given by the Cid should be returned, and that the heirs of Carrion together with one of their kindred should do battle against three knights of the party of the Cid. The guilty youths would have declined the combat; but all their shifts were in vain. They were vanquished in the lists, and forever disgraced, while their injured wives were sought in marriage by great princes.

Some Spanish writers have labored to show, by an examination of dates and circumstances, that this story is untrue. Such confutation was surely not needed; for the narrative is on the face of it a romance. How it found its way into Mariana's history is quite clear. He acknowledges his obligations to the ancient chronicles; and had doubtless before him the Cronica del famoso Cavallero Cid Ruy Diez Campeador, which had been printed as early as the year 1552. He little suspected that all the most striking passages in this chronicle were copied from a poem of the twelfth century,— a poem of which the language and versification had long been obsolete, but which glowed with no common portion of the fire of the Iliad. Yet such is the fact. More than a century and a half after the death of Mariana, this venerable ballad, of which one imperfect copy on parchment, four hundred years old, had been preserved at Bivar, was for the first time printed. Then it was found that every interesting circumstance of the story of the heirs of Carrion was derived by the eloquent Jesuit from a song of which he had never heard, and which was composed by a minstrel whose very name had been long forgotten.

Such, or nearly such, appears to have been the process by which the lost ballad-poetry of Rome was transformed into history. To reverse that process, to transform some portions of early Roman history back into the poetry out of which they were made, is the object of this work.

In the following poems the author speaks, not in his own person, but in the persons of ancient minstrels who know only what a Roman citizen, born three or four hundred years before the Christian era, may be supposed to have known, and who are in no wise above the passions and prejudices of their age and nation. To these imaginary poets must be ascribed some blunders which are so obvious that is unnecessary to point them out. The real blunder would have been to represent these old poets as deeply versed in general history, and studious of chronological accuracy. To them must also be attributed the illiberal sneers at the Greeks, the furious party spirit, the contempt for the arts of peace, the love of war for its own sake, the ungenerous exultation over the vanquished, which the reader will sometimes observe. To portray a Roman of the age of Camillus or Curius as superior to national antipathies, as mourning over the devastation and slaughter by which empire and triumphs were to be won, as looking on human suffering with the sympathy of Howard or as treating conquered enemies with the delicacy of the Black Prince, would be to violate all dramatic propriety. The old Romans had some great virtues, fortitude, temperance, veracity, spirit to resist oppression, respect for legitimate authority, fidelity in the observing of contracts, disinterestedness, ardent patriotism; but Christian charity and chivalrous generosity were alike unknown to them.

It would have been obviously improper to mimic the manner of any particular age or country. Something has been borrowed however, from our own old ballads, and more from Sir Walter Scott the great restorer of our ballad-poetry. To the Iliad still greater obligations are due; and those obligations have been contracted with the less hesitation, because there is reason to believe that some of the old Latin minstrels really had recourse to that inexhaustible store of poetical images.

It would have been easy to swell this little volume to a very considerable bulk, by appending notes filled with quotations; but to a learned reader such notes are not necessary; for an unlearned reader they would have little interest; and the judgment passed both by the learned and by the unlearned on a work of the imagination will always depend much more on the general character and spirit of such a work than on minute details.

HORATIUS

There can be little doubt that among those parts of early Roman history which had a poetical origin was the legend of Horatius Cocles. We have several versions of the story, and these versions differ from each other in points of no small importance. Polybius, there is reason to believe, heard the tale recited over the remains of some Consul or Prætor descended from the old Horatian patricians; for he introduces it as a specimen of the narratives with which the Romans were in the habit of embellishing their funeral oratory. It is remarkable that, according to him, Horatius defended the bridge alone, and perished in the waters. According to the chronicles which Livy and Dionysius followed, Horatius had two companions, swam safe to shore, and was loaded with honors and rewards.

These discrepancies are easily explained. Our own literature, indeed, will furnish an exact parallel to what may have taken place at Rome. It is highly probably that the memory of the war of Porsena was preserved by compositions much resembling the two ballads which stand first in the Relics of Ancient English Poetry. In both those ballads the English, commanded by the Percy, fight with the Scots, commanded by the Douglas. In one of the ballads the Douglas is killed by a nameless English archer, and the Percy by a Scottish spearman; in the other, the Percy slays the Douglas in single combat, and is himself made prisoner. In the former, Sir Hugh Montgomery is shot through the heart by a Northumbrian bowman; in the latter he is taken and exchanged for the Percy. Yet both the ballads relate to the same event, and that event which probably took place within the memory of persons who were alive when both the ballads were made. One of the Minstrels says:—

> "Old men that knowen the grounde well yenoughe
> Call it the battell of Otterburn:
> At Otterburn began this spurne
> Upon a monnyn day.
> Ther was the dougghte Doglas slean:
> The Perse never went away."

The other poet sums up the event in the following lines:

> "Thys fraye bygan at Otterborne
> Bytwene the nyghte and the day:

> *Ther the Doglas lost hys lyfe,*
> *And the Percy was lede away."*

It is by no means unlikely that there were two old Roman lays about the defence of the bridge; and that, while the story which Livy has transmitted to us was preferred by the multitude, the other, which ascribed the whole glory to Horatius alone, may have been the favorite with the Horatian house.

The following ballad is supposed to have been made about a hundred and twenty years after the war which it celebrates, and just before the taking of Rome by the Gauls. The author seems to have been an honest citizen, proud of the military glory of his country, sick of the disputes of factions, and much given to pining after good old times which had never really existed. The allusion, however, to the partial manner in which the public lands were allotted could proceed only from a plebeian; and the allusion to the fraudulent sale of spoils marks the date of the poem, and shows that the poet shared in the general discontent with which the proceedings of Camullus, after the taking of Veii, were regarded.

The penultimate syllable of the name Porsena has been shortened in spite of the authority of Niebuhr, who pronounces, without assigning any ground for his opinion, that Martial was guilty of a decided blunder in the line,

> *"Hanc spectare manum Porsena non potuit."*

It is not easy to understand how any modern scholar, whatever his attainments may be,— and those of Niebuhr were undoubtedly immense,— can venture to pronounce that Martial did not know the quantity of a word which he must have uttered, and heard uttered, a hundred times before he left school. Niebuhr seems also to have forgotten that Martial has fellow culprits to keep him in countenance. Horace has committed the same decided blunder; for he give us, as a pure iambic line,—

> *"Minacis aut Etrusca Porsenæ dextram;"*

Silius Italicus has repeatedly offended in the same way, as when he says,— "Clusinum vulgus, cum, Porsena magne, jubebas." A modern writer may be content to err in such company.

Niebuhr's supposition that each of the three defenders of the bridge was the representative of one of the three patrician tribes is both ingenious and probable, and has been adopted in the following poem.

Horatius

A Lay Made About the Year Of The City CCCLX

I

Lars Porsena of Closium
   By the Nine Gods he swore
That the great house of Tarquin
   Should suffer wrong no more.
By the Nine Gods he swore it,
   And named a trysting day,
And bade his messengers ride forth,
East and west and south and north,
   To summon his array.

II

East and west and south and north
   The messengers ride fast,
And tower and town and cottage
   Have heard the trumpet's blast.
Shame on the false Etruscan
   Who lingers in his home,
When Porsena of Clusium
   Is on the march for Rome.

III

The horsemen and the footmen
   Are pouring in amain
From many a stately market-place,
   From many a fruitful plain,
From many a lonely hamlet,
   Which, hid by beech and pine,
Like an eagle's nest, hangs on the crest
   Of purple Apennine;

IV

From lordly Volaterræ,
   Where scowls the far-famed hold

- 15 -

Piled by the hands of giants
　　For godlike kings of old;
From seagirt Populonia,
　　Whose sentinels descry
Sardinia's snowy mountain-tops
　　Fringing the southern sky;

V

From the proud mart of Pisæ,
　　Queen of the western waves,
Where ride Massilia's triremes
　　Heavy with fair-haired slaves;
From where sweet Clanis wanders
　　Through corn and vines and flowers;
From where Cortona lifts to heaven
　　Her diadem of towers.

VI

Tall are the oaks whose acorns
　　Drop in dark Auser's rill;
Fat are the stags that champ the boughs
　　Of the Ciminian hill;
Beyond all streams Clitumnus
　　Is to the herdsman dear;
Best of all pools the fowler loves
　　The great Volsinian mere.

VII

But now no stroke of woodman
　　Is heard by Auser's rill;
No hunter tracks the stag's green path
　　Up the Ciminian hill;
Unwatched along Clitumnus
　　Grazes the milk-white steer;
Unharmed the water fowl may dip
　　In the Volsminian mere.

VIII

The harvests of Arretium,
　　This year, old men shall reap;
This year, young boys in Umbro
　　Shall plunge the struggling sheep;
And in the vats of Luna,
　　This year, the must shall foam

Round the white feet of laughing girls
    Whose sires have marched to Rome.

IX

There be thirty chosen prophets,
    The wisest of the land,
Who alway by Lars Porsena
    Both morn and evening stand:
Evening and morn the Thirty
    Have turned the verses o'er,
Traced from the right on linen white
    By mighty seers of yore.

X

And with one voice the Thirty
    Have their glad answer given:
"Go forth, go forth, Lars Porsena;
    Go forth, beloved of Heaven;
Go, and return in glory
    To Clusium's royal dome;
And hang round Nurscia's altars
    The golden shields of Rome."

XI

And now hath every city
    Sent up her tale of men;
The foot are fourscore thousand,
    The horse are thousands ten.
Before the gates of Sutrium
    Is met the great array.
A proud man was Lars Porsena
    Upon the trysting day.

XII

For all the Etruscan armies
    Were ranged beneath his eye,
And many a banished Roman,
    And many a stout ally;
And with a mighty following
    To join the muster came
The Tusculan Mamilius,
    Prince of the Latin name.

XIII

But by the yellow Tiber
    Was tumult and affright:
From all the spacious champaign
    To Rome men took their flight.
A mile around the city,
    The throng stopped up the ways;
A fearful sight it was to see
    Through two long nights and days.

XIV

For aged folks on crutches,
    And women great with child,
And mothers sobbing over babes
    That clung to them and smiled,
And sick men borne in litters
    High on the necks of slaves,
And troops of sun-burned husbandmen
    With reaping-hooks and staves,

XV

And droves of mules and asses
    Laden with skins of wine,
And endless flocks of goats and sheep,
    And endless herds of kine,
And endless trains of wagons
    That creaked beneath the weight
Of corn-sacks and of household goods,
    Choked every roaring gate.

XVI

Now, from the rock Tarpeian,
    Could the wan burghers spy
The line of blazing villages
    Red in the midnight sky.
The Fathers of the City,
    They sat all night and day,
For every hour some horseman come
    With tidings of dismay.

XVII

To eastward and to westward
    Have spread the Tuscan bands;

Nor house, nor fence, nor dovecote
    In Crustumerium stands.
Verbenna down to Ostia
    Hath wasted all the plain;
Astur hath stormed Janiculum,
    And the stout guards are slain.
        XVIII

I wis, in all the Senate,
    There was no heart so bold,
But sore it ached, and fast it beat,
    When that ill news was told.
Forthwith up rose the Consul,
    Up rose the Fathers all;
In haste they girded up their gowns,
    And hied them to the wall.

        XIX

They held a council standing,
    Before the River-Gate;
Short time was there, ye well may guess,
    For musing or debate.
Out spake the Consul roundly:
    "The bridge must straight go down;
For, since Janiculum is lost,
    Nought else can save the town."

        XX

Just then a scout came flying,
    All wild with haste and fear:
"To arms! to arms! Sir Consul:
    Lars Porsena is here."
On the low hills to westward
    The Consol fixed his eye,
And saw the swarthy storm of dust
    Rise fast along the sky.

        XXI

And nearer fast and nearer
    Doth the red whirlwind come;
And louder still and still more loud,
From underneath that rolling cloud,
Is heard the trumpet's war-note proud,
    The trampling, and the hum.
And plainly and more plainly

Now through the gloom appears,
Far to left and far to right,
In broken gleams of dark-blue light,
The long array of helmets bright,
    The long array of spears.

XXII

And plainly and more plainly,
    Above that glimmering line,
Now might ye see the banners
    Of twelve fair cities shine;
But the banner of proud Clusium
    Was highest of them all,
The terror of the Umbrian,
    The terror of the Gaul.

XXIII

And plainly and more plainly
    Now might the burghers know,
By port and vest, by horse and crest,
    Each warlike Lucumo.
There Cilnius of Arretium
    On his fleet roan was seen;
And Astur of the four-fold shield,
Girt with the brand none else may wield,
Tolumnius with the belt of gold,
And dark Verbenna from the hold
    By reedy Thrasymene.

XXIV

Fast by the royal standard,
    O'erlooking all the war,
Lars Porsena of Clusium
    Sat in his ivory car.
By the right wheel rode Mamilius,
    Prince of the Latian name;
And by the left false Sextus,
    That wrought the deed of shame.

XXV

But when the face of Sextus
    Was seen among the foes,
A yell that rent the firmament
    From all the town arose.

On the house-tops was no woman
But spat towards him and hissed,
No child but screamed out curses,
And shook its little fist.

XXVI

But the Consul's brow was sad,
And the Consul's speech was low,
And darkly looked he at the wall,
And darkly at the foe.
"Their van will be upon us
Before the bridge goes down;
And if they once may win the bridge,
What hope to save the town?"

XXVII

Then out spake brave Horatius,
The Captain of the Gate:
"To every man upon this earth
Death cometh soon or late.
And how can man die better
Than facing fearful odds,
For the ashes of his fathers,
And the temples of his gods,

XXVIII

"And for the tender mother
Who dandled him to rest,
And for the wife who nurses
His baby at her breast,
And for the holy maidens
Who feed the eternal flame,
To save them from false Sextus
That wrought the deed of shame?

XXIX

"Haul down the bridge, Sir Consul,
With all the speed ye may;
I, with two more to help me,
Will hold the foe in play.
In yon strait path a thousand
May well be stopped by three.
Now who will stand on either hand,
And keep the bridge with me?"

XXX

Then out spake Spurius Lartius;
A Ramnian proud was he:
"Lo, I will stand at thy right hand,
And keep the bridge with thee."
And out spake strong Herminius;
Of Titian blood was he:
"I will abide on thy left side,
And keep the bridge with thee."

XXXI

"Horatius," quoth the Consul,
"As thou sayest, so let it be."
And straight against that great array
Forth went the dauntless Three.
For Romans in Rome's quarrel
Spared neither land nor gold,
Nor son nor wife, nor limb nor life,
In the brave days of old.

XXXII

Then none was for a party;
Then all were for the state;
Then the great man helped the poor,
And the poor man loved the great:
Then lands were fairly portioned;
Then spoils were fairly sold:
The Romans were like brothers
In the brave days of old.

XXXIII

Now Roman is to Roman
More hateful than a foe,
And the Tribunes beard the high,
And the Fathers grind the low.
As we wax hot in faction,
In battle we wax cold:
Wherefore men fight not as they fought
In the brave days of old.

XXXIV

Now while the Three were tightening
Their harness on their backs,

The Consul was the foremost man
    To take in hand an axe:
And Fathers mixed with Commons
    Seized hatchet, bar, and crow,
And smote upon the planks above,
    And loosed the props below.

XXXV

Meanwhile the Tuscan army,
    Right glorious to behold,
Come flashing back the noonday light,
Rank behind rank, like surges bright
    Of a broad sea of gold.
Four hundred trumpets sounded
    A peal of warlike glee,
As that great host, with measured tread,
And spears advanced, and ensigns spread,
Rolled slowly towards the bridge's head,
    Where stood the dauntless Three.

XXXVI

The Three stood calm and silent,
    And looked upon the foes,
And a great shout of laughter
    From all the vanguard rose:
And forth three chiefs came spurring
    Before that deep array;
To earth they sprang, their swords they drew,
And lifted high their shields, and flew
    To win the narrrow way;

XXXVII

Aunus from green Tifernum,
    Lord of the Hill of Vines;
And Seius, whose eight hundred slaves
    Sicken in Ilva's mines;
And Picus, long to Clusium
    Vassal in peace and war,
Who led to fight his Umbrian powers
From that gray crag where, girt with towers,
The fortress of Nequinum lowers
    O'er the pale waves of Nar.

XXXVIII

Stout Lartius hurled down Aunus
    Into the stream beneath;
Herminius struck at Seius,
    And clove him to the teeth;
At Picus brave Horatius
    Darted one fiery thrust;
And the proud Umbrian's gilded arms
    Clashed in the bloody dust.

XXXIX

Then Ocnus of Falerii
    Rushed on the Roman Three;
And Lausulus of Urgo,
    The rover of the sea;
And Aruns of Volsinium,
    Who slew the great wild boar,
The great wild boar that had his den
Amidst the reeds of Cosa's fen,
And wasted fields, and slaughtered men,
    Along Albinia's shore.

XL

Herminius smote down Aruns:
    Lartius laid Ocnus low:
Right to the heart of Lausulus
    Horatius sent a blow.
"Lie there," he cried, "fell pirate!
    No more, aghast and pale,
From Ostia's walls the crowd shall mark
The track of thy destroying bark.
No more Campania's hinds shall fly
To woods and caverns when they spy
    Thy thrice accursed sail."

XLI

But now no sound of laughter
    Was heard among the foes.
A wild and wrathful clamor
    From all the vanguard rose.
Six spears' lengths from the entrance
    Halted that deep array,
And for a space no man came forth
    To win the narrow way.

XLII

But hark! the cry is Astur:
    And lo! the ranks divide;
And the great Lord of Luna
    Comes with his stately stride.
Upon his ample shoulders
    Clangs loud the four-fold shield,
And in his hand he shakes the brand
    Which none but he can wield.

XLIII

He smiled on those bold Romans
    A smile serene and high;
He eyed the flinching Tuscans,
    And scorn was in his eye.
Quoth he, "The she-wolf's litter
    Stand savagely at bay:
But will ye dare to follow,
    If Astur clears the way?"

XLIV

Then, whirling up his broadsword
    With both hands to the height,
He rushed against Horatius,
    And smote with all his might.
With shield and blade Horatius
    Right deftly turned the blow.
The blow, though turned, came yet too nigh;
It missed his helm, but gashed his thigh:
The Tuscans raised a joyful cry
    To see the red blood flow.

XLV

He reeled, and on Herminius
    He leaned one breathing-space;
Then, like a wild cat mad with wounds,
    Sprang right at Astur's face.
Through teeth, and skull, and helmet
    So fierce a thrust he sped,
The good sword stood a hand-breadth out
    Behind the Tuscan's head.

XLVI

And the great Lord of Luna
   Fell at that deadly stroke,
As falls on Mount Alvernus
   A thunder smitten oak:
Far o'er the crashing forest
   The giant arms lie spread;
And the pale augurs, muttering low,
   Gaze on the blasted head.

XLVII

On Astur's throat Horatius
   Right firmly pressed his heel,
And thrice and four times tugged amain,
   Ere he wrenched out the steel.
"And see," he cried, "the welcome,
   Fair guests, that waits you here!
What noble Lucomo comes next
   To taste our Roman cheer?"

XLVIII

But at his haughty challenge
   A sullen murmur ran,
Mingled of wrath, and shame, and dread,
   Along that glittering van.
There lacked not men of prowess,
   Nor men of lordly race;
For all Etruria's noblest
   Were round the fatal place.

XLIX

But all Etruria's noblest
   Felt their hearts sink to see
On the earth the bloody corpses,
   In the path the dauntless Three:
And, from the ghastly entrance
   Where those bold Romans stood,
All shrank, like boys who unaware,
Ranging the woods to start a hare,
Come to the mouth of the dark lair
Where, growling low, a fierce old bear
   Lies amidst bones and blood.

L

Was none who would be foremost
    To lead such dire attack;
But those behind cried, "Forward!"
    And those before cried, "Back!"
And backward now and forward
    Wavers the deep array;
And on the tossing sea of steel
To and frow the standards reel;
And the victorious trumpet-peal
    Dies fitfully away.

LI

Yet one man for one moment
    Strode out before the crowd;
Well known was he to all the Three,
    And they gave him greeting loud.
"Now welcome, welcome, Sextus!
    Now welcome to thy home!
Why dost thou stay, and turn away?
    Here lies the road to Rome.

LII

Thrice looked he at the city;
    Thrice looked he at the dead;
And thrice came on in fury,
    And thrice turned back in dread:
And, white with fear and hatred,
    Scowled at the narrow way
Where, wallowing in a pool of blood,
    The bravest Tuscans lay.

LIII

But meanwhile axe and lever
    Have manfully been plied;
And now the bridge hangs tottering
    Above the boiling tide.
"Come back, come back, Horatius!"
    Loud cried the Fathers all.
"Back, Lartius! back, Herminius!
    Back, ere the ruin fall!"

LIV

Back darted Spurius Lartius;
Herminius darted back:
And, as they passed, beneath their feet
They felt the timbers crack.
But when they turned their faces,
And on the farther shore
Saw brave Horatius stand alone,
They would have crossed once more.

LV

But with a crash like thunder
Fell every loosened beam,
And, like a dam, the mighty wreck
Lay right athwart the stream:
And a long shout of triumph
Rose from the walls of Rome,
As to the highest turret-tops
Was splashed the yellow foam.

LVI

And, like a horse unbroken
When first he feels the rein,
The furious river struggled hard,
And tossed his tawny mane,
And burst the curb and bounded,
Rejoicing to be free,
And whirling down, in fierce career,
Battlement, and plank, and pier,
Rushed headlong to the sea.

LVII

Alone stood brave Horatius,
But constant still in mind;
Thrice thirty thousand foes before,
And the broad flood behind.
"Down with him!" cried false Sextus,
With a smile on his pale face.
"Now yield thee," cried Lars Porsena,
"Now yield thee to our grace."

LVIII

Round turned he, as not deigning

Those craven ranks to see;
Nought spake he to Lars Porsena,
    To Sextus nought spake he;
But he saw on Palatinus
    The white porch of his home;
And he spake to the noble river
    That rolls by the towers of Rome.

LVIX

"Oh, Tiber! Father Tiber!
    To whom the Romans pray,
A Roman's life, a Roman's arms,
    Take thou in charge this day!"
So he spake, and speaking sheathed
    The good sword by his side,
And with his harness on his back,
    Plunged headlong in the tide.

LX

No sound of joy or sorrow
    Was heard from either bank;
But friends and foes in dumb surprise,
With parted lips and straining eyes,
    Stood gazing where he sank;
And when above the surges,
    They saw his crest appear,
All Rome sent forth a rapturous cry,
And even the ranks of Tuscany
    Could scarce forbear to cheer.

LXI

But fiercely ran the current,
    Swollen high by months of rain:
And fast his blood was flowing;
    And he was sore in pain,
And heavy with his armor,
    And spent with changing blows:
And oft they thought him sinking,
    But still again he rose.

LXII

Never, I ween, did swimmer,
    In such an evil case,
Struggle through such a raging flood

Safe to the landing place:
But his limbs were borne up bravely
    By the brave heart within,
And our good father Tiber
    Bare bravely up his chin.

LXIII

"Curse on him!" quoth false Sextus;
    "Will not the villain drown?
But for this stay, ere close of day
    We should have sacked the town!"
"Heaven help him!" quoth Lars Porsena
    "And bring him safe to shore;
For such a gallant feat of arms
    Was never seen before."

LXIV

And now he feels the bottom;
    Now on dry earth he stands;
Now round him throng the Fathers;
    To press his gory hands;
And now, with shouts and clapping,
    And noise of weeping loud,
He enters through the River-Gate
    Borne by the joyous crowd.

LXV

They gave him of the corn-land,
    That was of public right,
As much as two strong oxen
    Could plough from morn till night;
And they made a molten image,
    And set it up on high,
And there is stands unto this day
    To witness if I lie.

LXVI

It stands in the Comitium
    Plain for all folk to see;
Horatius in his harness,
    Halting upon one knee:
And underneath is written,
    In letters all of gold,

How valiantly he kept the bridge
   In the brave days of old.

LXVII

And still his name sounds stirring
   Unto the men of Rome,
As the trumpet-blast that cries to them
   To charge the Volscian home;
And wives still pray to Juno
   For boys with hearts as bold
As his who kept the bridge so well
   In the brave days of old.

LXVIII

And in the nights of winter,
   When the cold north winds blow,
And the long howling of the wolves
   Is heard amidst the snow;
When round the lonely cottage
   Roars loud the tempest's din,
And the good logs of Algidus
   Roar louder yet within;

LXIX

When the oldest cask is opened,
   And the largest lamp is lit;
When the chestnuts glow in the embers,
   And the kid turns on the spit;
When young and old in circle
   Around the firebrands close;
When the girls are weaving baskets,
   And the lads are shaping bows;

LXX

When the goodman mends his armor,
   And trims his helmet's plume;
When the goodwife's shuttle merrily
   Goes flashing through the loom;
With weeping and with laughter
   Still is the story told,
How well Horatius kept the bridge
   In the brave days of old.

THE BATTLE OF THE LAKE REGILLUS

The following poem is supposed to have been produced about ninety years after the lay of Horatius. Some persons mentioned in the lay of Horatius make their appearance again, and some appellations and epithets used in the lay of Horatius have been purposely repeated: for, in an age of ballad-poetry, it scarcely ever fails to happen, that certain phrases come to be appropriated to certain men and things, and are regularly applied to those men and things by every minstrel. Thus we find, both in the Homeric poems and in Hesiod, [several examples of common phrases, in Greek]. Thus, too, in our own national songs, Douglas is almost always the doughty Douglas; England is merry England; all the gold is red; and all the ladies are gay.

The principal distinction between the lay of Horatius and the lay of the Lake Regillus is that the former is meant to be purely Roman, while the latter, though national in its general spirit, has a slight tincture of Greek learning and of Greek superstition. The story of the Tarquins, as it has come down to us, appears to have been compiled from the works of several popular poets; and one, at least of those poets appears to have visited the Greek colonies in Italy, if not Greece itself, and to have had some acquaintance with the works of Homer and Herodotus. Many of the most striking adventures of the House of Tarquin, before Lucretia makes her appearance, have a Greek character. The Tarquins themselves are represented as Corinthian nobles of the great House of the Bacchiadæ, driven from their country by the tyranny of that Cypselus, the tale of whose strange escape Herodotus has related with incomparable simplicity and liveliness. Livy and Dionysius tell us that, when Tarquin the Proud was asked what was the best mode of governing a conquered city, he replied only by beating down with his staff all the tallest poppies in his garden. This is exactly what Herodotus, in the passage to which reference has already been made, relates of the counsel given to Periander, the son of Cypselus. The stratagem by which the town of Gabii is brought under the power of the Tarquins is, again, obviously copied from Herodotus. The embassy of the young Tarquins to the oracle at Delphi is just such a story as would be told by a poet whose head was full of the Greek mythology; and the ambiguous answer returned by Apollo is in the exact style of the prophecies which, according to Herodotus, lured Croesus to destruction. Then the character of the narrative changes. From the first mention of Lucretia to the retreat of Porsena nothing seems to be borrowed from foreign sources. The villainy of Sextus, the suicide of his victim, the revolution, the death of the sons of Brutus, the defence of the bridge, Musius burning his hand, Cloelia swimming through Tiber, seem to be all strictly Roman. But when we have done with the Tuscan wars, and enter upon the war with the Latines, we are again struck by the Greek air of the story. The Battle of the Lake Regillus is in all respects a Homeric battle, except that the combatants ride astride on their horses, instead of driving chariots. The mass of fighting men is hardly mentioned. The leaders single each other out, and engage hand to hand. The great object of the warriors on both sides is, as in the Iliad, to obtain possession of the spoils and bodies of the slain; and several circumstances are related which forcibly remind us of the great slaughter round the corpses of Sarpedon and Patroclus.

But there is one circumstance which deserves especial notice. Both the war of Troy and the war of Regillus were caused by the licentious passions of young princes, who were therefore peculiarly bound not to be sparing of their own persons on the day of battle. Now the conduct of Sextus at Regillus, as described by Livy, so exactly resembles that of Paris, as described at the beginning of the third book of the Iliad, that it is difficult to believe the resemblance accidental. Paris appears before the Trojan ranks, defying the bravest Greek to encounter him:—

3 lines from the Iliad, in Greek, probably those
translated by Pope as:

...to the van, before the sons of fame
Whom Troy sent forth, the beauteous Paris came:

Livy introduces Sextus in a similar manner: "Ferocem juvenem Tarquinium, ostentantem se in prima exsulum acie." Menelaus rushes to meet Paris. A Roman noble, eager for vengeance, spurs his horse towards Sextus. Both the guilty princes are instantly terror-stricken:—

3 more lines in Greek, Pope's translation being:

...[Menelaus] approaching near,

> *The beauteous champion views with marks of fear,*
> *Smit with a conscious sense, retires behind,*
> *And shuns the fate he well deserv'd to find.*

"Tarquinius," says Livy, "retro in agmen suorum infenso cessit hosti." If this be a fortuitous coincidence, it is also one of the most extraordinary in literature.

In the following poem, therefore, images and incidents have been borrowed, not merely without scruple, but on principle, from the incomparable battle-pieces of Homer.

The popular belief at Rome, from an early period, seems to have been that the event of the great day of Regillus was decided by supernatural agency. Castor and Pollux, it was said, had fought armed and mounted, at the head of the legions of the commonwealth, and had afterwards carried the news of the victory with incredible speed to the city. The well in the Forum at which they had alighted was pointed out. Near the well rose their ancient temple. A great festival was kept to their honor on the Ides of Quintilis, supposed to be the anniversary of the battle; and on that day sumptuous sacrifices were offered to them at the public charge. One spot on the margin of Lake Regillus was regarded during many ages with superstitious awe. A mark, resembling in shape a horse's hoof, was discernible in the volcanic rock; and this mark was believed to have been made by one of the celestial chargers.

How the legend originated cannot now be ascertained; but we may easily imagine several ways in which it might have originated; nor is it at all necessary to suppose, with Julius Frontinus, that two young men were dressed up by the Dictator to personate the sons of Leda. It is probable that Livy is correct when he says that the Roman general, in the hour of peril, vowed a temple to Castor. If so, nothing could be more natural than that the multitude should ascribe the victory to the favor of the Twin Gods. When such was the prevailing sentiment, any man who chose to declare that, in the midst of the confusion and slaughter, he had seen two godlike forms on white horses scattering the Latines, would find ready credence. We know indeed, that in modern times a very similar story actually found credence among a people much more civilized than the Romans of the fifth century before Christ. A chaplain of Cortes, writing about thirty years after the conquest of Mexico, in an age of printing presses, libraries, universities, scholars, logicians, jurists, and statesmen, had the face to assert that, in one engagement against the

Indians, St. James had appeared on a gray horse at the head of the Castilian adventurers. Many of those adventurers were living when this lie was printed. One of them, honest Bernal Diaz, wrote an account of the expedition. He had the evidence of his own senses against the legend; but he seems to have distrusted even the evidence of his own senses. He says that he was in the battle, and that he saw a gray horse with a man on his back, but that the man was, to his thinking, Francesco de Morla, and not the ever-blessed apostle St. James. "Nevertheless," Bernal adds, "it may be that the person on the gray horse was the glorious apostle St. James, and that I, sinner that I am, was unworthy to see him." The Romans of the age of Cincinatus were probably quite as credulous as the Spanish subjects of Charles the Fifth. It is therefore conceivable that the appearance of Castor and Pollux may be become an article of faith before the generation which had fought at Regillus had passed away. Nor could anything be more natural than that the poets of the next age should embellish this story, and make the celestial horsemen bear the tidings of victory to Rome.

Many years after the temple of the Twin Gods had been built in the Forum, an important addition was made to the ceremonial by which the state annually testified its gratitude for their protection. Quintus Fabius and Publius Decius were elected Censors at a momentous crisis. It had become absolutely necessary that the classification of the citizens should be revised. On that classification depended the distribution of political power. Party spirit ran high; and the republic seemed to be in danger of falling under the dominion either of a narrow oligarchy or of an ignorant and headstrong rabble. Under such circumstances, the most illustrious patrician and the most illustrious plebeian of the age were entrusted with the office of arbitrating between the angry factions; and they performed their arduous task to the satisfaction of all honest and reasonable men.

One of their reforms was the remodelling of the equestrian order; and, having effected this reform, they determined to give to their work a sanction derived from religion. In the chivalrous societies of modern times,— societies which have much more than may at first sight appear in common with with the equestrian order of Rome,— it has been usual to invoke the special protection of some Saint, and to observe his day with peculiar solemnity. Thus the Companions of the Garter wear the image of St. George depending from their collars, and meet, on great occasions, in St. George's Chapel. Thus, when Louis the Fourteenth instituted a new order of chivalry for the rewarding of military merit, he commended it to the favor of his own glorified ancestor and patron, and decreed that all the members of the fraternity should meet at the royal palace on the feast of St. Louis, should attend the king to chapel, should hear mass, and should subsequently hold their great annual assembly. There is a considerable resemblance between this rule of the order of St. Louis and the rule which Fabius and Decius made respecting the Roman knights. It was ordained that a grand muster and inspection of the equestrian body should be part of the ceremonial performed, on the anniversary of the battle of Regillus, in honor of Castor and Pollux the two equestrian gods. All the knights, clad in purple and crowned with olive, were to meet at a temple of Mars in the suburbs. Thence they were to ride in state to the Forum, where the temple of the Twins stood. This pageant was, during several centuries, considered as one of the most splendid sights of Rome. In the time of Dionysius the cavalcade sometimes consisted of five thousand horsemen, all persons of fair repute and easy fortune.

There can be no doubt that the Censors who instituted this august ceremony acted in concert with the Pontiffs to whom, by the constitution of Rome, the superintendence of the public worship belonged; and it is probable that those high religious functionaries were, as usual, fortunate enough to find in their books or traditions some warrant for the innovation.

The following poem is supposed to have been made for this great occasion. Songs, we know, were chanted at religious festivals of Rome from an early period, indeed from so early a period that some of the sacred verses were popularly ascribed to Numa, and were utterly unintelligible in the age of Augustus. In the Second Punic War a great feast was held in honor of Juno, and a song was sung in her praise. This song was extant when Livy wrote; and, though exceedingly rugged and uncouth, seemed to him not wholly destitute of merit. A song, as we learn from Horace, was part of the established ritual at the great Secular Jubilee. It is therefore likely that the Censors and Pontiffs, when they had resolved to add a grand procession of knights to the other solemnities annually performed on the Ides of Quintilis, would call in the aid of a poet. Such a poet would naturally take for his subject the battle of Regillus, the appearance of the Twin Gods, and the institution of their festival. He would find abundant materials in the ballads of his predecessors; and he would make free use of the scanty stock of Greek learning which he had himself acquired. He would probably introduce some wise and holy Pontiff enjoining the magnificent ceremonial which, after a long interval, had at length been adopted. If the poem succeeded, many persons would commit it to memory. Parts of it would be sung to the pipe at banquets. It would be peculiarly interesting to the great Posthumian House, which numbered among its many images that of the Dictator Aulus, the hero of Regillus. The orator who, in the following generation, pronounced the funeral panegyric over the remains of Lucius Posthumius Megellus, thrice Consul, would borrow largely from the lay; and thus some passages, much disfigured, would probably find their way into the chronicles which were afterwards in the hands of Dionysius and Livy.

Antiquaries differ widely as to the situation of the field of battle. The opinion of those who suppose that the armies met near Cornufelle, between Frascati and the Monte Porzio, is at least plausible, and has been followed in the poem.

As to the details of the battle, it has not been thought desirable to adhere minutely to the accounts which have come down to us. Those accounts, indeed, differ widely from each other, and, in all probability, differ as widely from the ancient poem from which they were originally derived.

It is unnecessary to point out the obvious imitations of the Iliad, which have been purposely introduced.

The Battle of the Lake Regillus
A Lay Sung at the Feast of Castor and Pollux on the Ides of
Quintilis in the year of the City CCCCLI.

I

Ho, trumpets, sound a war-note!
    Ho, lictors, clear the way!
The Knights will ride, in all their pride,
    Along the streets to-day.
To-day the doors and windows
    Are hung with garlands all,
From Castor in the Forum,
    To Mars without the wall.
Each Knight is robed in purple,
    With olive each is crowned;
A gallant war-horse under each

Paws haughtily the ground.
While flows the Yellow River,
  While stands the Sacred Hill,
The proud Ides of Quintilis
  Shall have such honor still.
Gay are the Martian Kalends,
  December's Nones are gay,
But the proud Ides, when the squadron rides,
  Shall be Rome's whitest day.

II

Unto the Great Twin Brethren
  We keep this solemn feast.
Swift, swift, the Great Twin Brethren
  Came spurring from the east.
They came o'er wild Parthenius
  Tossing in waves of pine,
O'er Cirrha's dome, o'er Adria's foam,
  O'er purple Apennine,
From where with flutes and dances
  Their ancient mansion rings,
In lordly Lacedæmon,
  The City of two kings,
To where, by Lake Regillus,
  Under the Porcian height,
All in the lands of Tusculum,
  Was fought the glorious fight.

III

Now on the place of slaughter
  Are cots and sheepfolds seen,
And rows of vines, and fields of wheat,
  And apple-orchards green;
The swine crush the big acorns
  That fall from Corne's oaks.
Upon the turf by the Fair Fount
  The reaper's pottage smokes.
The fisher baits his angle;
  The hunter twangs his bow;
Little they think on those strong limbs
  That moulder deep below.
Little they think how sternly
  That day the trumpets pealed;
How in the slippery swamp of blood
  Warrior and war-horse reeled;
How wolves came with fierce gallops,

And crows on eager wings,
To tear the flesh of captains,
And peck the eyes of kings;
How thick the dead lay scattered
Under the Porcian height;
How through the gates of Tusculum
Raved the wild stream of flight;
And how the Lake Regillus
Bubbled with crimson foam,
What time the Thirty Cities
Came forth to war with Rome.

IV

But Roman, when thou standest
Upon that holy ground,
Look thou with heed on the dark rock
That girds the dark lake round.
So shalt thou see a hoof-mark
Stamped deep into the flint:
It was not hoof of mortal steed
That made so strange a dint:
There to the Great Twin Brethren
Vow thou thy vows, and pray
That they, in tempest and in flight,
Will keep thy head alway.

V

Since last the Great Twin Brethren
Of mortal eyes were seen,
Have years gone by an hundred
And fourscore and thirteen.
That summer a Virginius
Was Consul first in place;
The second was stout Aulus,
Of the Posthumian race.
The Herald of the Latines
From Gabii came in state:
The Herald of the Latines
Passed through Rome's Eastern Gate:
The Herald of the Latines
Did in our Forum stand;
And there he did his office,
A sceptre in his hand.

VI

"Hear, Senators and people
    Of the good town of Rome,
The Thirty Cities charge you
    To bring the Tarquins home:
And if ye still be stubborn
    To work the Tarquins wrong,
The Thirty Cities warn you,
    Look your walls be strong."

VII

Then spake the Consul Aulus,
    He spake a bitter jest:
"Once the jays sent a message
    Unto the eagle's nest:—
Now yield thou up thine eyrie
    Unto the carrion-kite,
Or come forth valiantly, and face
    The jays in deadly fight.—
Forth looked in wrath the eagle;
    And carrion-kite and jay,
Soon as they saw his beak and claw,
    Fled screaming far away."

VIII

The Herald of the Latines
    Hath hied him back in state:
The Fathers of the City
    Are met in high debate.
Then spake the elder Consul,
    And ancient man and wise:
"Now harken, Conscript Fathers,
    To that which I advise.
In seasons of great peril
    'Tis good that one bear sway;
Then choose we a Dictator,
    Whom all men shall obey.
Camerium knows how deeply
    The sword of Aulus bites,
And all our city calls him
    The man of seventy fights.
Then let him be Dictator
    For six months and no more,
And have a Master of the Knights,
    And axes twenty-four."

IX

So Aulus was Dictator,
    The man of seventy fights;
He made Æbutius Elva
    His Master of the Knights.
On the third morn thereafter,
    At downing of the day,
Did Aulus and Æbutius
    Set forth with their array.
Sempronius Atratinus
    Was left in charge at home
With boys, and with gray-headed men,
    To keep the walls of Rome.
Hard by the Lake Regillus
    Our camp was pitched at night:
Eastward a mile the Latines lay,
    Under the Porcian height.
Far over hill and valley
    Their mighty host was spread;
And with their thousand watch-fires
    The midnight sky was red.

X

Up rose the golden morning
    Over the Porcian height,
The proud Ides of Quintilis
    Marked evermore in white.
Not without secret trouble
    Our bravest saw the foe;
For girt by threescore thousand spears,
    The thirty standards rose.
From every warlike city
    That boasts the Latian name,
Fordoomed to dogs and vultures,
    That gallant army came;
From Setia's purple vineyards,
    From Norba's ancient wall,
From the white streets of Tusculum,
    The proudest town of all;
From where the Witch's Fortress
    O'er hangs the dark-blue seas;
From the still glassy lake that sleeps
    Beneath Aricia's trees—
Those trees in whose dim shadow
    The ghastly priest doth reign,
The priest who slew the slayer,

And shall himself be slain;
From the drear banks of Ufens,
    Where flights of marsh-fowl play,
And buffaloes lie wallowing
    Through the hot summer's day;
From the gigantic watch-towers,
    No work of earthly men,
Whence Cora's sentinels o'erlook
    The never-ending fen;
From the Laurentian jungle,
    The wild hog's reedy home;
From the green steeps whence Anio leaps
    In floods of snow-white foam.

XI

Aricia, Cora, Norba,
    Velitræ, with the might
Of Setia and of Tusculum,
    Were marshalled on the right:
The leader was Mamilius,
    Prince of the Latian name;
Upon his head a helmet
    Of red gold shone like flame:
High on a gallant charger
    Of dark-gray hue he rode;
Over his gilded armor
    A vest of purple flowed,
Woven in the land of sunrise
    By Syria's dark-browed daughters,
And by the sails of Carthage brought
    Far o'er the southern waters.

XII

Lavinium and Laurentum
    Had on the left their post,
With all the banners of the marsh,
    And banners of the coast.
Their leader was false Sextus,
    That wrought the deed of shame:
With restless pace and haggard face
    To his last field he came.
Men said he saw strange visions
    Which none beside might see;
And that strange sounds were in his ears
    Which none might hear but he.
A woman fair and stately,

But pale as are the dead,
Oft through the watches of the night
    Sat spinning by his bed.
And as she plied the distaff,
    In a sweet voice and low,
She sang of great old houses,
    And fights fought long ago.
So spun she, and so sang she,
    Until the east was gray.
Then pointed to her bleeding breast,
    And shrieked, and fled away.

XIII

But in the centre thickest
    Were ranged the shields of foes,
And from the centre loudest
    The cry of battle rose.
There Tibur marched and Pedum
    Beneath proud Tarquin's rule,
And Ferentinum of the rock,
    And Gabii of the pool.
There rode the Volscian succors:
    There, in the dark stern ring,
The Roman exiles gathered close
    Around the ancient king.
Though white as Mount Soracte,
    When winter nights are long,
His beard flowed down o'er mail and belt,
    His heart and hand were strong:
Under his hoary eyebrows
    Still flashed forth quenchless rage:
And, if the lance shook in his gripe,
    'Twas more with hate than age.
Close at his side was Titus
    On an Apulian steed,
Titus, the youngest Tarquin,
    Too good for such a breed.

XIV

Now on each side the leaders
    Gave signal for the charge;
And on each side the footmen
    Strode on with lance and targe;
And on each side the horsemen
    Struck their spurs deep in gore,
And front to front the armies

Met with a mighty roar:
And under that great battle
The earth with blood was red;
And, like the Pomptine fog at morn,
The dust hung overhead;
And louder still and louder
Rose from the darkened field
The braying of the war-horns,
The clang of sword and shield,
The rush of squadrons sweeping
Like whirlwinds o'er the plain,
The shouting of the slayers,
And screeching of the slain.

XV

False Sextus rode out foremost,
His look was high and bold;
His corslet was of bison's hide,
Plated with steel and gold.
As glares the famished eagle
From the Digentian rock
On a choice lamb that bounds alone
Before Bandusia's flock,
Herminius glared on Sextus,
And came with eagle speed,
Herminius on black Auster,
Brave champion on brave steed;
In his right hand the broadsword
That kept the bridge so well,
And on his helm the crown he won
When proud Fidenæ fell.
Woe to the maid whose lover
Shall cross his path to-day!
False Sextus saw, and trembled,
And turned, and fled away.
As turns, as flies, the woodman
In the Calabrian brake,
When through the reeds gleams the round eye
Of that fell speckled snake;
So turned, so fled, false Sextus,
And hid him in the rear,
Behind the dark Lavinian ranks,
Bristling with crest and spear.

XVI

But far to the north Æbutius,

The Master of the Knights,
Gave Tubero of Norba
    To feed the Porcian kites.
Next under those red horse-hoofs
    Flaccus of Setia lay;
Better had he been pruning
    Among his elms that day.
Mamilus saw the slaughter,
    And tossed his golden crest,
And towards the Master of the Knights
    Through the thick battle pressed.
Æbutius smote Mamilius
    So fiercely on the shield
That the great lord of Tusculum
    Well-nigh rolled on the field.
Mamilius smote Æbutius,
    With a good aim and true,
Just where the next and shoulder join,
    And pierced him through and through;
And brave Æbutius Elva
    Fell swooning to the ground:
But a thick wall of bucklers
    Encompassed him around.
His clients from the battle
    Bare him some little space,
And filled a helm from the dark lake,
    And bathed his brow and face;
And when at last he opened
    His swimming eyes to light,
Men say, the earliest words he spake
    Was, "Friends, how goes the fight?".

XVII

But meanwhile in the centre
    Great deeds of arms were wrought;
There Aulus the Dictator
    And there Valerius fought.
Aulus with his good broadsword
    A bloody passage cleared
To where, amidst the thickest foes,
    He saw the long white beard.
Flat lighted that good broadsword
    Upon proud Tarquin's head.
He dropped the lance: he dropped the reins:
    He fell as fall the dead.
Down Aulus springs to slay him,
    With eyes like coals of fire;

But faster Titus hath sprung down,
    And hath bestrode his sire.
Latian captains, Roman knights,
    Fast down to earth they spring,
And hand to hand they fight on foot
    Around the ancient king.
First Titus gave tall Cæso
    A death wound in the face;
Tall Cæso was the bravest man
    Of the brave Fabian race:
Aulus slew Rex of Gabii,
    The priest of Juno's shrine;
Valerius smote down Julius,
    Of Rome's great Julian line;
Julius, who left his mansion,
    High on the Velian hill,
And through all turns of weal and woe
    Followed proud Tarquin still.
Now right across proud Tarquin
    A corpse was Julius laid;
And Titus groaned with rage and grief,
    And at Valerius made.
Valerius struck at Titus,
    And lopped off half his crest;
But Titus stabbed Valerius
    A span deep in the breast.
Like a mast snapped by the tempest,
    Valerius reeled and fell.
Ah! woe is me for the good house
    That loves the people well!
Then shouted loud the Latines;
    And with one rush they bore
The struggling Romans backward
    Three lances' length and more:
And up they took proud Tarquin,
    And laid him on a shield,
And four strong yeomen bare him,
    Still senseless, from the field.

XVIII

But fiercer grew the fighting
    Around Valerius dead;
For Titus dragged him by the foot
    And Aulus by the head.
"On, Latines, on!" quoth Titus,
    "See how the rebels fly!"
"Romans, stand firm!" quoth Aulus,

"And win this fight or die!
They must not give Valerius
    To raven and to kite;
For aye Valerius loathed the wrong,
    And aye upheld the right:
And for your wives and babies
    In the front rank he fell.
Now play the men for the good house
    That loves the people well!"

XIX

Then tenfold round the body
    The roar of battle rose,
Like the roar of a burning forest,
    When a strong north wind blows,
Now backward, and now forward,
    Rocked furiously the fray,
Till none could see Valerius,
    And none wist where he lay.
For shivered arms and ensigns
    Were heaped there in a mound,
And corpses stiff, and dying men
    That writhed and gnawed the ground;
And wounded horses kicking,
    And snorting purple foam:
Right well did such a couch befit
    A Consular of Rome.

XX

But north looked the Dictator;
    North looked he long and hard,
And spake to Caius Cossus,
    The Captain of his Guard;
"Caius, of all the Romans
    Thou hast the keenest sight,
Say, what through yonder storm of dust
    Comes from the Latian right;"

XXI

Then answered Caius Cossus:
    "I see an evil sight;
The banner of proud Tusculum
    Comes from the Latian right;
I see the pluméd horsemen;
    And far before the rest

I see the dark-gray charger,
    I see the purple vest;
I see the golden helmet
    That shines far off like flame;
So ever rides Mamilius,
    Prince of the Latian name."

XXII

"Now hearken, Caius Cossus:
    Spring on thy horse's back;
Ride as the wolves of Apennine
    Were all upon thy track;
Haste to our southward battle:
    And never draw thy rein
Until thou find Herminius,
    And bid hime come amain."

XXIII

So Aulus spake, and turned him
    Again to that fierce strife;
And Caius Cossus mounted,
    And rode for death and life.
Loud clanged beneath his horse-hoofs
    The helmets of the dead,
And many a curdling pool of blood
    Splashed him heel to head.
So came he far to southward,
    Where fought the Roman host,
Against the banners of the marsh
    And banners of the coast.
Like corn before the sickle
    The stout Laninians fell,
Beneath the edge of the true sword
    That kept the bridge so well.

XXIV

"Herminius! Aulus greets thee;
    He bids thee come with speed,
To help our central battle,
    For sore is there our need;
There wars the youngest Tarquin,
    And there the Crest of Flame,
The Tusculan Mamilius,
    Prince of the Latian name.
Valerius hath fallen fighting

In front of our array;
And Aulus of the seventy fields
  Alone upholds the day."

XXV

Herminius beat his bosom:
  But never a word he spake.
He clapped his hand on Auster's mane,
  He gave the reins a shake.
Away, away, went Auster,
  Like an arrow from the bow:
Black Auster was the fleetest steed
  From Aufidus to Po.

XXVI

Right glad were all the Romans
  Who, in that hour of dread,
Against great odds bare up the war
  Around Valerius dead,
When from the south the cheering
  Rose with a mighty swell;
"Herminius comes, Herminius,
  Who kept the bridge so well!"

XXVII

Mamilius spied Herminius,
  And dashed across the way.
"Herminius! I have sought thee
  Through many a bloody day.
One of us two, Herminius,
  Shall never more go home.
I will lay on for Tusculum,
  And lay thou on for Rome!"

XXVIII

All round them paused the battle,
  While met in mortal fray
The Roman and the Tusculan,
  The horses black and gray.
Herminius smote Mamilius
  Through breast-plate and through breast,
And fast flowed out the purple blood
  Over the purple vest.
Mamilius smote Herminius

> *Through head-piece and through head,*
> *And side by side those chiefs of pride,*
> *Together fell down dead.*
> *Down fell they dead together*
> *In a great lake of gore;*
> *And still stood all who saw them fall*
> *While men might count a score.*

XXIX

> *Fast, fast, with heels wild spurning,*
> *The dark-gray charger fled:*
> *He burst through ranks of fighting men,*
> *He sprang o'er heaps of dead.*
> *His bridle far out-streaming,*
> *His flanks all blood and foam,*
> *He sought the southern mountains,*
> *The mountains of his home.*
> *The pass was steep and rugged,*
> *The wolves they howled and whined;*
> *But he ran like a whirlwind up the pass,*
> *And he left the wolves behind.*
> *Through many a startled hamlet*
> *Thundered his flying feet;*
> *He rushed through the gate of Tusculum,*
> *He rushed up the long white street;*
> *He rushed by tower and temple,*
> *And paused not from his race*
> *Till he stood before his master's door*
> *In the stately market-place.*
> *And straightway round him gathered*
> *A pale and trembling crowd,*
> *And when they knew him, cries of rage*
> *Brake forth, and wailing loud:*
> *And women rent their tresses*
> *For their great prince's fall;*
> *And old men girt on their old swords,*
> *And went to man the wall.*

XXX

> *But, like a graven image,*
> *Black Auster kept his place,*
> *And ever wistfully he looked*
> *Into his master's face.*
> *The raven-mane that daily,*
> *With pats and fond caresses,*
> *The young Herminia washed and combed,*

And twined in even tresses,
And decked with colored ribbons
    From her own gay attire,
Hung sadly o'er her father's corpse
    In carnage and in mire.
Forth with a shout sprang Titus,
    And seized black Auster's rein.
Then Aulus sware a fearful oath,
    And ran at him amain.
"The furies of thy brother
    With me and mine abide,
If one of your accursed house
    Upon black Auster ride!"
As on a Alpine watch-tower
    From heaven comes down the flame,
Full on the neck of Titus
    The blade of Aulus came:
And out the red blood spouted,
    In a wide arch and tall,
As spouts a fountain in the court
    Of some rich Capuan's hall.
The knees of all the Latines
    Were loosened with dismay,
When dead, on dead Herminius,
    The bravest Tarquin lay.

XXXI

And Aulus the Dictator
    Stroked Auster's raven mane,
With heed he looked unto the girths,
    With heed unto the rein.
"Now bear me well, black Auster,
    Into yon thick array;
And thou and I will have revenge
    For thy good lord this day."

XXXII

So spake he; and was buckling
    Tighter black Auster's band,
When he was aware of a princely pair
    That rode at his right hand.
So like they were, no mortal
    Might one from other know:
White as snow their armor was:
    Their steeds were white as snow.
Never on earthly anvil

Did such rare armor gleam;
   And never did such gallant steeds
   Drink of an earthly stream.

XXXIII

And all who saw them trembled,
   And pale grew every cheek;
And Aulus the Dictator
   Scarce gathered voice to speak.
"Say by what name men call you?
   What city is your home?
And wherefore ride ye in such guise
   Before the ranks of Rome?"

XXXIV

"By many names men call us;
   In many lands we dwell:
Well Samothracia knows us;
   Cyrene knows us well.
Our house in gay Tarentum
   Is hung each morn with flowers:
High o'er the masts of Syracuse
   Our marble portal towers;
But by the proud Eurotas
   Is our dear native home;
And for the right we come to fight
   Before the ranks of Rome."

XXXV

So answered those strange horsemen,
   And each couched low his spear;
And forthwith all the ranks of Rome
   Were bold, and of good cheer:
And on the thirty armies
   Came wonder and affright,
And Ardea wavered on the left,
   And Cora on the right.
"Rome to the charge!" cried Aulus;
   "The foe begins to yield!
Charge for the hearth of Vesta!
   Charge for the Golden Shield!
Let no man stop to plunder,
   But slay, and slay, and slay;
The gods who live forever
   Are on our side to-day."

XXXVI

Then the fierce trumpet-flourish
    From earth to heaven arose,
The kites know well the long stern swell
    That bids the Romans close.
Then the good sword of Aulus
    Was lifted up to slay;
Then, like a crag down Apennine,
    Rushed Auster through the fray.
But under those strange horsemen
    Still thicker lay the slain;
And after those strange horses
    Black Auster toiled in vain.
Behind them Rome's long battle
    Came rolling on the foe,
Ensigns dancing wild above,
    Blades all in line below.
So comes the Po in flood-time
    Upon the Celtic plain;
So comes the squall, blacker than night,
    Upon the Adrian main.
Now, by our Sire Quirinus,
    It was a goodly sight
To see the thirty standards
    Swept down the tide of flight.
So flies the spray of Adria
    When the black squall doth blow
So corn-sheaves in the flood-time
    Spin down the whirling Po.
False Sextus to the mountains
    Turned first his horse's head;
And fast fled Ferentinum,
    And fast Lanuvium fled.
The horsemen of Nomentus
    Spurred hard out of the fray;
The footmen of Velitræ
    Threw shield and spear away.
And underfoot was trampled,
    Amidst the mud and gore,
The banner of proud Tusculum,
    That never stooped before:
And down went Flavius Faustus,
    Who led his stately ranks
From where the apple blossoms wave
    On Anio's echoing banks,
And Tullus of Arpinum,
    Chief of the Volscian aids,

And Metius with the long fair curls,
　　The love of Anxur's maids,
And the white head of Vulso,
　　The great Arician seer,
And Nepos of Laurentum
　　The hunter of the deer;
And in the back false Sextus
　　Felt the good Roman steel,
And wriggling in the dust he died,
　　Like a worm beneath the wheel:
And fliers and pursuers
　　Were mingled in a mass;
And far away the battle
　　Went roaring through the pass.

XXXVII

Semponius Atratinus
　　Sat in the Eastern Gate,
Beside him were three Fathers,
　　Each in his chair of state;
Fabius, whose nine stout grandsons
　　That day were in the field,
And Manlius, eldest of the Twelve
　　Who keep the Golden Shield;
And Sergius, the High Pontiff,
　　For wisdom far renowned;
In all Etruria's colleges
　　Was no such Pontiff found.
And all around the portal,
　　And high above the wall,
Stood a great throng of people,
　　But sad and silent all;
Young lads and stooping elders
　　That might not bear the mail,
Matrons with lips that quivered,
　　And maids with faces pale.
Since the first gleam of daylight,
　　Sempronius had not ceased
To listen for the rushing
　　Of horse-hoofs from the east.
The mist of eve was rising,
　　The sun was hastening down,
When he was aware of a princely pair
　　Fast pricking towards the town.
So like they were, man never
　　Saw twins so like before;
Red with gore their armor was,

Their steeds were red with gore.

XXXVIII

"Hail to the great Asylum!
Hail to the hill-tops seven!
Hail to the fire that burns for aye,
And the shield that fell from heaven!
This day, by Lake Regillus,
Under the Porcian height,
All in the lands of Tusculum
Was fought a glorious fight.
Tomorrow your Dictator
Shall bring in triumph home
The spoils of thirty cities
To deck the shrines of Rome!"

XXXIX

Then burst from that great concourse
A shout that shook the towers,
And some ran north, and some ran south,
Crying, "The day is ours!"
But on rode these strange horsemen,
With slow and lordly pace;
And none who saw their bearing
Durst ask their name or race.
On rode they to the Forum,
While laurel-boughs and flowers,
From house-tops and from windows,
Fell on their crests in showers.
When they drew nigh to Vesta,
They vaulted down amain,
And washed their horses in the well
That springs by Vesta's fane.
And straight again they mounted,
And rode to Vesta's door;
Then, like a blast, away they passed,
And no man saw them more.

XL

And all the people trembled,
And pale grew every cheek;
And Sergius the High Pontiff
Alone found voice to speak:
"The gods who live forever
Have fought for Rome to-day!

These be the Great Twin Brethren
　　To whom the Dorians pray.
Back comes the chief in triumph,
　　Who, in the hour of fight,
Hath seen the Great Twin Brethren
　　In harness on his right.
Safe comes the ship to haven,
　　Through billows and through gales,
If once the Great Twin Brethren
　　Sit shining on the sails.
Wherefore they washed their horses
　　In Vesta's holy well,
Wherefore they rode to Vesta's door,
　　I know, but may not tell.
Here, hard by Vesta's temple,
　　Build we a stately dome
Unto the Great Twin Brethren
　　Who fought so well for Rome.
And when the months returning
　　Bring back this day of fight,
The proud Ides of Quintilis,
　　Marked evermore with white,
Unto the Great Twin Brethren
　　Let all the people throng,
With chaplets and with offerings,
　　With music and with song;
And let the doors and windows
　　Be hung with garlands all,
And let the knights be summoned
　　To Mars without the wall:
Thence let them ride in purple
　　With joyous trumpet-sound,
Each mounted on his war-horse,
　　And each with olive crowned;
And pass in solemn order
　　Before the sacred dome,
Where dwell the Great Twin Brethren
　　Who fought so well for Rome."

VIRGINIA

A collection consisting exclusively of war-songs would give an imperfect, or rather an erroneous, notion of the spirit of the old Latin ballads. The Patricians, during more than a century after the expulsion of the Kings, held all the high military commands. A Plebeian, even though, like Lucius Siccius, he were distinguished by his valor and knowledge of war, could serve only in subordinate posts. A minstrel, therefore, who wished to celebrate the early triumphs of his country, could hardly take any but Patricians for his heroes. The warriors who are mentioned in the two preceding lays, Horatius, Lartius, Herminius, Aulus Posthumius, Æbutius Elva, Sempronius Atratinus, Valerius Poplicola, were all members of the dominant order; and a poet who was singing their praises, whatever his own political opinions might be, would naturally abstain from insulting the class to which they belonged, and from reflecting on the system which had placed such men at the head of the legions of the Commonwealth.

But there was a class of compositions in which the great families were by no means so courteously treated. No parts of early Roman history are richer with poetical coloring than those which relate to the long contest between the privileged houses and the commonality. The population of Rome was, from a very early period, divided into hereditary castes, which, indeed, readily united to repel foreign enemies, but which regarded each other, during many years, with bitter animosity. Between those castes there was a barrier hardly less strong than that which, at Venice, parted the members of the Great Council from their countrymen. In some respects, indeed, the line which separated an Icilius or a Duilius from a Posthumius or a Fabius was even more deeply marked than that which separated the rower of gondola from a Contarini or a Morosini. At Venice the distinction was merely civil. At Rome it was both civil and religious. Among the grievances under which the Plebeians suffered, three were felt as peculiarly severe. They were excluded from the highest magistracies; they were excluded from all share in the public lands; and they were ground down to the dust by partial and barbarous legislation touching pecuniary contracts. The ruling class in Rome was a moneyed class; and it made and administered the laws with a view solely to its own interest. Thus the relation between lender and borrower was mixed up with the relation between sovereign and subject. The great men held a large portion of the community in dependence by means of advances at enormous usury. The law of debt, framed by creditors, and for the protection of creditors, was the host horrible that has ever been known among men. The liberty and even the life of the insolvent were at the mercy of the Patrician money-lenders. Children often became slaves in consequence of the misfortunes of their parents. The debtor was imprisoned, not in a public jail under the care of impartial public functionaries, but in a private workhouse belonging to the creditor. Frightful stories were told respecting these dungeons. It was said that torture and brutal violation were common; that tight stocks, heavy chains, scanty measures of food, were used to punish wretches guilty of nothing but poverty; and that brave soldiers, whose breasts were covered with honorable scars, were often marked still more deeply on the back by the scourges of high-born usurers.

The Plebeians were, however, not wholly without constitutional rights. From an early period they had been admitted to some share of political power. They were enrolled each in his century, and were allowed a share, considerable though not proportioned to their numerical strength, in the disposal of those high dignities from which they were themselves excluded. Thus their position bore some resemblance to that of the Irish Catholics during the interval between the year 1792 and the year 1829. The Plebeians had also the privilege of annually appointing officers, named Tribunes, who had no active share in the government of the commonwealth, but who, by degree, acquired a power formidable even to the ablest and most resolute Consuls and Dictators. The person of the Tribune was inviolable; and, though he could directly effect little, he could obstruct everything.

During more than a century after the institution of the Tribuneship, the Commons struggled manfully for the removal of the grievances under which they labored; and, in spite of many checks and reverses, succeeded in wringing concession after concession from the stubborn aristocracy. At length in the year of the city 378, both parties mustered their whole strength for their last and most desperate conflict. The popular and active Tribune, Caius Licinius, proposed the three memorable laws which are called by his name, and which were intended to redress the three great evils of which the Plebeians complained. He was supported, with eminent ability and firmness, by his colleague, Lucius Sextius. The struggle appears to have been the fiercest that every in any community terminated without an appeal to arms. If such a contest had raged in any Greek city, the streets would have run with blood. But, even in the paroxysms of faction, the Roman retained his gravity, his respect for law, and his tenderness for the lives of his fellow citizens. Year after year Licinius and Sextius were reëlected Tribunes. Year after year, if the narrative which has come down to us is to be trusted, they continued to exert, to the full extent, their power of stopping the whole machine of government. No curule magistrates could be chosen; no military muster could be held. We know too little of the state of Rome in those days to be able to conjecture how, during that long anarchy, the peace was kept, and ordinary justice administered between man and man. The animosity of both parties rose to the greatest height. The excitement, we may well suppose, would have been peculiarly intense at the annual election of Tribunes. On such occasions there can be little doubt that the great families did all that could be done, by threats and caresses, to break the union of the Plebeians. That union, however, proved indissoluble. At length the good cause triumphed. The Licinian laws were carried. Lucius Sextius was the first Plebeian Consul, Caius Licinius the third.

The results of this great change were singularly happy and glorious. Two centuries of prosperity, harmony, and victory followed the reconciliation of the orders. Men who remembered Rome engaged in waging petty wars almost within sight of the Capitol lived to see her the mistress of Italy. While the disabilities of the Plebeians continued, she was scarcely able to maintain her ground against Volscians and Hernicans. When those disabilities were removed, she rapidly became more than a match for Carthage and Macedon.

During the great Licinian contest the Plebeian poets were, doubtless, not silent. Even in modern times songs have been by no means without influence on public affairs; and we may therefore infer that, in a society where printing was unknown and where books were rare, a pathetic or humorous party-ballad must have produced effects such as we can but faintly conceive. It is certain that satirical poems were common at Rome from a very early period. The rustics, who lived at a distance from the seat of government, and took little part in the strife of factions, gave vent to their petty local animosities in coarse Fescennine verse. The lampoons of the city were doubtless of a higher order; and their sting was early felt by the nobility. For in the Twelve Tables, long before the time of the Licinian laws, a severe punishment was denounced against the citizen who should compose or recite verses reflecting on another. Satire is, indeed, the only sort of composition in which the Latin poets, whose works have come down to us, were not mere imitators of foreign models; and it is therefore the only sort of composition in which they have never been rivalled. It was not, like their tragedy, their comedy, their epic and lyric poetry, a hothouse plant which, in return for assiduous and skilful culture, gave only scanty and sickly fruits. It was hardy and full of sap; and in all the various juices which it yielded might be distinguished the flavor of the Ausonian soil. "Satire," said Quinctilian, with just pride, "is all our own." Satire sprang, in truth, naturally from the constitution of the Roman government and from the spirit of the Roman people; and, though at length subjected to metrical rules derived from Greece, retained to the last an essentially Roman character. Lucilius was the earliest satirist whose works were held in esteem under the Caesars. But many years before Lucilius was born, Nævius had been flung into a dungeon, and guarded there with circumstances of unusual rigor, on account of the bitter lines in which he had attacked the great Caecilian family. The genius and spirit of the Roman satirists survived the liberty of their country, and were not extinguished by the cruel despotism of the Julian and Flavian Emperors. The great poet who told the story of Domitian's turbot was the legitimate successor of those forgotten minstrels whose songs animated the factions of the infant Republic.

Those minstrels, as Niebuhr has remarked, appear to have generally taken the popular side. We can hardly be mistaken in supposing that, at the great crisis of the civil conflict, they employed themselves in versifying all the most powerful and virulent speeches of the Tribunes, and in heaping abuse on the leaders of the aristocracy. Every personal defect, every domestic scandal, every tradition dishonorable to a noble house, would be sought out, brought into notice, and exaggerated. The illustrious head of the aristocratical party, Marcus Furius Camillus, might perhaps be, in some measure, protected by his venerable age and by the memory of his great services to the state. But Appius Claudius Crassus enjoyed no such immunity. He was descended from a long line of ancestors distinguished by their haughty demeanor, and by the inflexibility with which they had withstood all the demands of the Plebeian order. While the political conduct and the deportment of the Claudian nobles drew upon them the fiercest public hatred, they were accused of wanting, if any credit is due to the early history of Rome, a class of qualities which, in a military commonwealth, is sufficient to cover a multitude of offences. The chiefs of the family appear to have been eloquent, versed in civil business, and learned after the fashion of their age; but in war they were not distinguished by skill or valor. Some of them, as if conscious where their weakness lay, had, when filling the highest magistracies, taken internal administration as their department of public business, and left the military command to their colleagues. One of them had been entrusted with an army, and had failed ignominiously. None of them had been honored with a triumph. None of them had achieved any martial exploit, such as those by which Lucius Quinctius Cincinnatus, Titus Quinctius Capitolinus, Aulus Cornelius Cossus, and, above all, the great Camillus, had extorted the reluctant esteem of the multitude. During the Licinian conflict, Appius Claudius Crassus signalized himself by the ability and severity with which he harangued against the two great agitators. He would naturally, therefore, be the favorite mark of the Plebeian satirists; nor would they have been at a loss to find a point on which he was open to attack.

His grandfather, called, like himself, Appius Claudius, had left a name as much detested as that Sextus Tarquinius. This elder Appius had been Consul more than seventy years before the introduction of the Licinian laws. By availing himself of a singular crisis in public feeling, he had obtained the consent of the Commons to the abolition of the Tribuneship, and had been the chief of that Council of Ten to which the whole direction of the state had been committed. In a new months his administration had become universally odious. It had been swept away by an irresistible outbreak of popular fury; and its memory was still held in abhorrence by the whole city. The immediate cause of the downfall of this execrable government was said to have been an attempt made by Appius Claudius upon the chastity of a beautiful young girl of humble birth. The story ran that the Decemvir, unable to succeed by bribes and solicitations, resorted to an outrageous act of tyranny. A vile dependent of the Claudian house laid claim to the damsel as his slave. The cause was brought before the tribunal of Appius. The wicked magistrate, in defiance of the clearest proofs, gave judgment for the claimant. But the girl's father, a brave soldier, saved her from servitude and dishonor by stabbing her to the heart in the sight of the whole Forum. That blow was the signal for a general explosion. Camp and city rose at once;

the Ten were pulled down; the Tribuneship was reëstablished; and Appius escaped the hands of the executioner only by a voluntary death.

It can hardly be doubted that a story so admirably adapted to the purposes both of the poet and of the demagogue would be eagerly seized upon by minstrels burning with hatred against the Patrician order, against the Claudian house, and especially against the grandson and namesake of the infamous Decemvir.

In order that the reader may judge fairly of these fragments of the lay of Virginia, he must imagine himself a Plebeian who has just voted for the reëlection of Sextius and Licinius. All the power of the Patricians has been exerted to throw out the two great champions of the Commons. Every Posthumius, Æmilius, and Cornelius has used his influence to the utmost. Debtors have been let out of the workhouses on condition of voting against the men of the people; clients have been posted to hiss and interrupt the favorite candidates; Appius Claudius Crassus has spoken with more than his usual eloquence and asperity: all has been in vain, Licinius and Sextius have a fifth time carried all the tribes: work is suspended; the booths are closed; the Plebeians bear on their shoulders the two champions of liberty through the Forum. Just at this moment it is announced that a great poet, a zealous adherent of the Tribunes, has made a new song which will cut the Claudian nobles to the heart. The crowd gathers round him, and calls on him to recite it. He takes his stand on the spot where, according to tradition, Virginia, more than seventy years ago, was seized by the pandar of Appius, and he begins his story.

Virginia

Fragments of a Lay Sung in the Forum on the Day Whereon Lucius Sextius Sextinus Lateranus and Caius Licinius Calvus Stolo Were Elected Tribunes of the Commons the Fifth Time, in the Year of the City CCCLXXXII.

> Ye good men of the Commons, with loving hearts and true,
> Who stand by the bold Tribunes that still have stood by you,
> Come, make a circle round me, and mark my tale with care,
> A tale of what Rome once hath borne, of what Rome yet may bear.
> This is no Grecian fable, of fountains running wine,
> Of maids with snaky tresses, or sailors turned to swine.
> Here, in this very Forum, under the noonday sun,
> In sight of all the people, the bloody deed was done.
> Old men still creep among us who saw that fearful day,

Just seventy years and seven ago, when the wicked Ten bare sway.

Of all the wicked Ten still the names are held accursed,
And of all the wicked Ten Appius Claudius was the worst.
He stalked along the Forum like King Tarquin in his pride:
Twelve axes waited on him, six marching on a side;
The townsmen shrank to right and left, and eyed askance with fear
His lowering brow, his curling mouth which always seemed to
sneer;
That brow of hate, that mouth of scorn, marks all the kindred
still;
For never was there Claudius yet but wished the Commons ill;
Nor lacks he fit attendance; for close behind his heels,
With outstretched chin and crouching pace, the client Marcus
steals,
His loins girt up to run with speed, be the errand what it may,
And the smile flickering on his cheek, for aught his lord may
say.
Such varlets pimp and jest for hire among the lying Greeks:
Such varlets still are paid to hoot when brave Licinius speaks.
Where'er ye shed the honey, the buzzing flies will crowd;
Where'er ye fling the carrion, the raven's croak is loud;
Where'er down Tiber garbage floats, the greedy pike ye see;
And wheresoe'er such lord is found, such client still will be.

Just then, as through one cloudless chink in a black stormy
sky
Shines out the dewy morning-star, a fair young girl came by.
With her small tablets in her hand, and her satchel on her arm,
Home she went bounding from the school, nor dreamed of shame
or harm;
And past those dreaded axes she innocently ran,
With bright frank brow that had not learned to blush at gaze of
man;
And up the Sacred Street she turned, and, as she danced along,
She warbled gayly to herself lines of the good old song,
How for a sport the princes came spurring from the camp,
And found Lucrece, combing the fleece, under the midnight lamp.
The maiden sang as sings the lark, when up he darts his flight,
From his nest in the green April corn, to meet the morning light;
And Appius heard her sweet young voice, and saw her sweet young
face,
And loved her with the accursed love of his accursed race,
And all along the Forum, and up the Sacred Street,
His vulture eye pursued the trip of those small glancing feet.

. . . .

Over the Alban mountains the light of morning broke;
From all the roofs of the Seven Hills curled the thin wreaths of
smoke:
The city-gates were opened; the Forum all alive
With buyers and with sellers was humming like a hive:
Blithely on brass and timber the craftsman's stroke was ringing,
And blithely o'er her panniers the market-girl was singing,
And blithely young Virginia came smiling from her home:
Ah! woe for young Virginia, the sweetest maid in Rome!
With her small tablets in her hand, and her satchel on her arm,
Forth she went bounding to the school, nor dreamed of shame or
harm.
She crossed the Forum shining with stalls in alleys gay,
And just had reached the very spot whereon I stand this day,
When up the varlet Marcus came; not such as when erewhile
He crouched behind his patron's heels with the true client smile:
He came with lowering forehead, swollen features, and clenched
fist,
And strode across Virginia's path, and caught her by the wrist.
Hard strove the frightened maiden, and screamed with look aghast,
And at her scream from right and left the folk came running fast;
The money-changer Crispus, with his thin silver hairs,
And Hanno from the stately booth glittering with Punic wares,
And the strong smith Muræna, grasping a half-forged brand,
And Volero the flesher, his cleaver in his hand.
All came in wrath and wonder, for all knew that fair child;
And, as she passed them twice a day, all kissed their hands and
smiled;
And the strong smith Muræna gave Marcus such a blow,
The caitiff reeled three paces back, and let the maiden go.
Yet glared he fiercely round him, and growled in harsh, fell
tone,
"She's mine, and I will have her, I seek but for mine own:
She is my slave, born in my house, and stolen away and sold,
The year of the sore sickness, ere she was twelve hours old.
'Twas in the sad September, the month of wail and fright,
Two augers were borne forth that morn; the Consul died ere night.
I wait on Appius Claudius, I waited on his sire:
Let him who works the client wrong beware the patron's ire."

So spake the varlet Marcus; and dread and silence came
On all the people at the sound of the great Claudian name.
For then there was no Tribune to speak the word of might,
Which makes the rich man tremble, and guards the poor man's
right.
There was no brave Licinius, no honest Sixtius then;
But all the city, in great fear, obeyed the wicked Ten.

Yet ere the varlet Marcus again might seize the maid,
Who clung tight to Muræna's skirt, and sobbed, and shrieked for aid,
Forth through the throng of gazers the young Icilius pressed,
And stamped his foot, and rent his gown, and smote upon his breast,
And sprang upon that column, by many a minstrel sung,
Whereon three mouldering helmets, three rusting swords, are hung,
And beckoned to the people, and in bold voice and clear
Poured thick and fast the burning words which tyrants quake to hear.

"Now, by your children's cradles, now by your fathers' graves,
Be men to-day, Quirites, or be forever slaves!
For this did Servius give us laws? For this did Lucrece bleed?
For this was the great vengeance wrought on Tarquin's evil seed?
For this did those false sons make red the axes of their sire?
For this did Scævola's right hand hiss in the Tuscan fire?
Shall the vile fox-earth awe the race that stormed the lion's den?
Shall we, who could not brook one lord, crouch to the wicked Ten?
Oh, for that ancient spirit which curbed the Senate's will!
Oh, for the tents which in old time whitened the Sacred Hill!
In those brave days our fathers stood firmly side by side;
They faced the Marcian fury; they tamed the Fabian pride:
They drove the fiercest Quinctius an outcast forth from Rome;
They sent the haughtiest Claudius with shivered fasces home.
But what their care bequeathed us our madness flung away:
All the ripe fruit of threescore years was blighted in a day.
Exult, ye proud Patricians! The hard-fought fight is o'er.
We strove for honors—'twas in vain; for freedom—'tis no more.
No crier to the polling summons the eager throng;
No Tribune breathes the word of might that guards the weak from wrong.
Our very hearts, that were so high, sink down beneath your will.
Riches, and lands, and power, and state—ye have them:—keep them still.
Still keep the holy fillets; still keep the purple gown,
The axes, and the curule chair, the car, and laurel crown:
Still press us for your cohorts, and, when the fight is done,
Still fill your garners from the soil which our good swords have won.
Still, like a spreading ulcer, which leech-craft may not cure,
Let your foul usance eat away the substance of the poor.
Still let your haggard debtors bear all their fathers bore;
Still let your dens of torment be noisome as of yore;
No fire when Tiber freezes; no air in dog-star heat;

And store of rods for free-born backs, and holes for free-born feet.
Heap heavier still the fetters; bar closer still the grate;
Patient as sheep we yield us up unto your cruel hate.
But, by the Shades beneath us, and by the gods above,
Add not unto your cruel hate your yet more cruel love!
Have ye not graceful ladies, whose spotless lineage springs
From Consuls, and High Pontiffs, and ancient Alban kings?
Ladies, who deign not on our paths to set their tender feet,
Who from their cars look down with scorn upon the wondering street,
Who in Corinthian mirrors their own proud smiles behold,
And breathe the Capuan odors, and shine with Spanish gold?
Then leave the poor Plebeian his single tie to life—
The sweet, sweet love of daughter, of sister, and of wife,
The gentle speech, the balm for all that his vexed soul endures,
The kiss, in which he half forgets even such a yoke as yours.
Still let the maiden's beauty swell the father's breast with pride;
Still let the bridegroom's arms infold an unpolluted bride.
Spare us the inexpiable wrong, the unutterable shame,
That turns the coward's heart to steel, the sluggard's blood to flame,
Lest, when our latest hope is fled, ye taste of our despair,
And learn by proof, in some wild hour, how much the wretched dare."

. . . .

. . . .

Straightway Virginius led the maid a little space aside,
To where the reeking shambles stood, piled up with horn and hide,
Close to yon low dark archway, where, in a crimson flood,
Leaps down to the great sewer the gurgling stream of blood.
Hard by, a flesher on a block had laid his whittle down:
Virginius caught the whittle up, and hid it in his gown.
And then his eyes grew very dim, and his throat began to swell,
And in a hoarse, changed voice he spake, "Farewell, sweet child! Farewell!
Oh! how I loved my darling! Though stern I sometimes be,
To thee, thou know'st, I was not so. Who could be so to thee?
And how my darling loved me! How glad she was to hear
My footstep on the threshold when I came back last year!
And how she danced with pleasure to see my civic crown,
And took my sword, and hung it up, and brought me forth my gown!
Now, all those things are over—yes, all thy pretty ways,

Thy needlework, thy prattle, thy snatches of old lays;
And none will grieve when I go forth, or smile when I return,
Or watch beside the old man's bed, or weep upon his urn.
The house that was the happiest within the Roman walls,
The house that envied not the wealth of Capua's marble halls,
Now, for the brightness of thy smile, must have eternal gloom,
And for the music of thy voice, the silence of the tomb.
The time is come. See how he points his eager hand this way!
See how his eyes gloat on thy grief, like a kite's upon the prey!
With all his wit, he little deems, that, spurned, betrayed,
bereft,
Thy father hath in his despair one fearful refuge left.
He little deems that in this hand I clutch what still can save
Thy gentle youth from taunts and blows, the portion of the slave;
Yea, and from nameless evil, that passeth taunt and blow—
Foul outrage which thou knowest not, which thou shalt never know.
Then clasp me round the neck once more, and give me one more
kiss;
And now mine own dear little girl, there is no way but this."
With that he lifted high the steel, and smote her in the side,
And in her blood she sank to earth, and with one sob she died.

    Then, for a little moment, all people held their breath;
And through the crowded Forum was stillness as of death;
And in another moment brake forth from one and all
A cry as if the Volscians were coming o'er the wall.
Some with averted faces shrieking fled home amain;
Some ran to call a leech; and some ran to lift the slain;
Some felt her lips and little wrist, if life might there be
found;
And some tore up their garments fast, and strove to stanch the
wound.
In vain they ran, and felt, and stanched; for never truer blow
That good right arm had dealt in fight agains a Volscian foe.

    When Appius Claudius saw that deed, he shuddered and sank
down,
And hid his face some little space with the corner of his gown,
Till, with white lips and bloodshot eyes, Virginius tottered
nigh,
And stood before the judgment-seat, and held the knife on high.
"Oh! dwellers in the nether gloom, avengers of the slain,
By this dear blood I cry to you, do right between us twain;
And even as Appius Claudius hath dealt by me and mine,
Deal you by Appius Claudius and all the Claudian line!"
So spake the slayer of his child, and turned, and went his way;
But first he cast one haggard glance to where the body lay,
And writhed, and groaned a fearful groan, an then, with steadfast

- 67 -

feet,
Strode right across the market-place unto the Sacred Street.

Then up sprang Appius Claudius: "Stop him; alive or dead!
Ten thousand pounds of copper to the man who brings his head."
He looked upon his clients; but none would work his will.
He looked upon his lictors, but they trembled, and stood still.
And, as Virginius through the press his way in silence cleft,
Ever the mighty multitude fell back to right and left.
And he hath passed in safety unto his woeful home,
And there ta'en horse to tell the camp what deeds are done in
Rome.

By this the flood of people was swollen from every side,
And streets and porches round were filled with that o'erflowing
tide;
And close around the body gathered a little train
Of them that were the nearest and dearest to the slain.
They brought a bier, and hung it with many a cypress crown,
And gently they uplifted her, and gently laid her down.
The face of Appius Claudius wore the Claudian scowl and sneer,
And in the Claudian note he cried, "What doth this rabble here?
Have they no crafts to mind at home, that hitherward they stray?
Ho! lictors, clear the market-place, and fetch the corpse away!"
The voice of grief and fury till then had not been loud;
But a deep sullen murmur wandered among the crowd,
Like the moaning noise that goes before the whirlwind on the
deep,
Or the growl of a fierce watch-dog but half aroused from sleep.
But when the lictors at that word, tall yeomen all and strong,
Each with his axe and sheaf of twigs, went down into the throng,
Those old men say, who saw that day of sorrow and of sin,
That in the Roman Forum was never such a din.
The wailing, hooting, cursing, the howls of grief and hate,
Were heard beyond the Pincian Hill, beyond the Latin Gate.
But close around the body, where stood the little train
Of them that were the nearest and dearest to the slain,
No cries were there, but teeth set fast, low whispers and black
frowns,
And breaking up of benches, and girding up of gowns.
'Twas well the lictors might not pierce to where the maiden lay,
Else surely had they been all twelve torn limb from limb that
day.
Right glad they were to struggle back, blood streaming from their
heads,
With axes all in splinters, and raiment all in shreds.
Then Appius Claudius gnawed his lip, and the blood left his
cheek,

And thrice he beckoned with his hand, and thrice he strove to
speak;
And thrice the tossing Forum set up a frightful yell:
"See, see, thou dog! what thou hast done; and hide thy shame in
hell!
Thou that wouldst make our maidens slaves must first make slaves
of men.
Tribunes! Hurrah for Tribunes! Down with the wicked Ten!"
And straightway, thick as hailstones, came whizzing through the
air,
Pebbles, and bricks, and potsherds, all round the curule chair:
And upon Appius Claudius great fear and trembling came,
For never was a Claudius yet brave against aught but shame.
Though the great houses love us not, we own, to do them right,
That the great houses, all save one, have borne them well in
fight.
Still Caius of Corioli, his triumphs and his wrongs,
His vengeance and his mercy, live in our camp-fire songs.
Beneath the yoke of Furius oft have Gaul and Tuscan bowed:
And Rome may bear the pride of him of whom herself is proud.
But evermore a Claudius shrinks from a stricken field,
And changes color like a maid at sight of sword and shield.
The Claudian triumphs all were won within the city towers;
The Claudian yoke was never pressed on any necks but ours.
A Cossus, like a wild cat, springs ever at the face;
A Fabius rushes like a boar against the shouting chase;
But the vile Claudian litter, raging with currish spite,
Still yelps and snaps at those who run, still runs from those who
smite.
So now 'twas seen of Appius. When stones began to fly,
He shook, and crouched, and wrung his hands, and smote upon his
thigh.
"Kind clients, honest lictors, stand by me in this fray!
Must I be torn in pieces? Home, home the nearest way!"
While yet he spake, and looked around with a bewildered stare,
Four sturdy lictors put their necks beneath the curule chair;
And fourscore clients on the left, and fourscore on the right,
Arrayed themselves with swords and staves, and loins girt up to
fight.
But, though without or staff or sword, so furious was the throng,
That scarce the train with might and main could bring their lord
along.
Twelve times the crowd made at him; five times they seized his
gown;
Small chance was his to rise again, if once they got him down:
And sharper came the pelting; and evermore the yell,—
"Tribunes! we will have Tribunes!"— rose with a louder swell:
And the chair tossed as tosses a bark with tattered sail

When raves the Adriatic beneath an eastern gale,
When Calabrian sea-marks are lost in clouds of spume,
And the great Thunder-Cape has donned his veil of inky gloom.
One stone hit Appius in the mouth, and one beneath the ear;
And ere he reached Mount Palatine, he swooned with pain and fear
His cursed head, that he was wont to hold so high with pride,
Now, like a drunken man's, hung down, and swayed from side to side;
And when his stout retainers had brought him to his door,
His face and neck were all one cake of filth and clotted gore.
As Appius Claudius was that day, so may his grandson be!
God send Rome one such other sight, and send me there to see!

THE PROPHECY OF CAPYS

It can hardly be necessary to remind any reader that according to the popular tradition, Romulus, after he had slain his granduncle Amulius, and restored his grandfather Numitor, determined to quit Alba, the hereditary domain of the Sylvian princes, and to found a new city. The gods, it was added, vouchsafed the clearest signs of the favor with which they regarded the enterprise, and of the high destinies reserved for the young colony.

This event was likely to be a favorite theme of the old Latin minstrels. They would naturally attribute the project of Romulus to some divine intimation of the power and prosperity which it was decreed that his city should attain. They would probably introduce seers foretelling the victories of unborn Consuls and Dictators, and the last great victory would generally occupy the most conspicuous place in the prediction. There is nothing strange in the supposition that the poet who was employed to celebrate the first great triumph of the Romans over the Greeks might throw his song of exultation into this form.

The occasion was one likely to excite the strongest feelings of national pride. A great outrage had been followed by a great retribution. Seven years before this time, Lucius Posthumius Megellus, who sprang from one of the noblest houses of Rome, and had been thrice Consul, was sent ambassador to Tarentum, with charge to demand reparation for grievous injuries. The Tarentines gave him audience in their theatre, where he addressed them in such Greek as he could command, which, we may well believe, was not exactly such as Cineas would have spoken. An exquisite sense of the ridiculous belonged to the Greek character; and closely connected with this faculty was a strong propensity to flippancy and impertinence. When Posthumius placed an accent wrong, his hearers burst into a laugh. When he remonstrated, they hooted him, and called him barbarian; and at length hissed him off the stage as if he had been a bad actor. As the grave Roman retired, a buffoon, who, from his constant drunkenness, was nicknamed the Pint-pot, came up with gestures of the grossest indecency, and bespattered the senatorial gown with filth. Posthumius turned round to the multitude, and held up the gown, as if appealing to the universal law of nations. The sight only increased the insolence of the Tarentines. They clapped their hands, and set up a shout of laughter which shook the theatre. "Men of Tarentum," said Posthumius, "it will take not a little blood to wash this gown."

Rome, in consequence of this insult, declared war against the Tarentines. The Tarentines sought for allies beyond the Ionian Sea Phyrrhus, king of Epirus, came to their help with a large army; and for the first time, the two great nations of antiquity were fairly matched against each other.

The fame of Greece in arms, as well as in arts, was then at the height. Half a century earlier, the career of Alexander had excited the admiration and terror of all nations from the Ganges to the Pillars of Hercules. Royal houses, founded by Macedonian captains, still reigned at Antioch and Alexandria. That barbarian warriors, led by barbarian chiefs, should win a pitched battle against Greek valor guided by Greek science, seemed as incredible as it would now seem that the Burmese or the Siamese should, in the open plain, put to flight an equal number of the best English troops. The Tarentines were convinced that their countrymen were irresistible in war; and this conviction had emboldened them to treat with the grossest indignity one whom they regarded as the representative of an inferior race. Of the Greek generals then living Pyrrhus was indisputably the first. Among the troops who were trained in the Greek discipline his Epirotes ranked high. His expedition to Italy was a turning-point in the history of the world. He found there a people who, far inferior to the Athenians and Corinthians in the fine arts, in the speculative sciences, and in all the refinements of life, were the best soldiers on the face of the earth. Their arms, their gradations of rank, their order of battle, their method of intrenchment, were all of Latin origin, and had all been gradually brought near to perfection, not by the study of foreign models, but by the genius and experience of many generations of great native commanders. The first words which broke from the king, when his practised eye had surveyed the Roman encampment, were full of meaning: "These barbarians," he said, "have nothing barbarous in their military arrangements." He was at first victorious; for his own talents were superior to those of the captains who were opposed to him; and the Romans were not prepared for the onset of the elephants of the East, which were then for the first time seen in Italy— moving mountains, with long snakes for hands. But the victories of the Epirotes were fiercely disputed, dearly purchased, and altogether unprofitable. At length, Manius Curius Dentatus, who had in his first Consulship won two triumphs, was again placed at the head of the Roman Commonwealth, and sent to conquer the invaders. A great battle was fought near Beneventum. Pyrrhus was completely defeated. He repassed the sea; and the world learned, with amazement, that a people had been discovered who, in fair fighting, were superior to the best troops that had been drilled on the system of Parmenio and Antigonus.

The conquerors had a good right to exult in their success; for their glory was all their own. They had not learned from their enemy how to conquer him. It was with their own national arms, and in their own national battle array, that they had overcome weapons and tactics long believed to be invincible. The pilum and the broadsword had vanquished the Macedonian spear. The legion had broken the Macedonian phalanx. Even the elephants, when the surprise produced by their first appearance was over, could cause no disorder in the steady yet flexible battalions of Rome. It is said by Florus, and may easily be believed, that the triumph far surpassed in magnificence any that Rome had previously seen. The only spoils which Papirius Cursor and Fabius Maximus could exhibit were flocks and herds, wagons of rude structure, and heaps of spears and helmets. But now, for the first time, the riches of Asia and the arts of Greece adorned a Roman pageant. Plate, fine stuffs, costly furniture, rare animals, exquisite paintings and sculptures, formed part of the procession. At the banquet would be assembled a crowd of warriors and statesmen, among whom Manius Curius Dentatus would take the highest room. Caius Fabricius Luscinus, then, after two Consulships and two triumphs, Censor of the Commonwealth, would doubtless occupy a place of honor at the board. In situations less conspicuous probably lay some of those who were, a few years later, the terror of Carthage: Caius Duilius, the founder of the maritime greatness of his country; Marcus Atilius Regulus, who owed to defeat a renown far higher than that which he had derived from his victories; and Caius Lutatius Catulus, who, while suffering from a grievous wound, fought the great battle of the Æates, and brought the First Punic War to a triumphant close. It is impossible to recount the names of these eminent citizens, without reflecting that they were, without exception, Plebeians, and would, but for the ever memorable struggle maintained by Caius Licinius and Lucius Sextius, have been doomed to hide in obscurity, or to waste in civil broils, the capacity and energy which prevailed against Pyrrhus and Hamilcar.

On such a day we may suppose that the patriotic enthusiasm of a Latin poet would vent itself in reiterated shouts of "Io triumphe," such as were uttered by Horace on a far less exciting occasion, and in boasts resembling those which Virgil put into the mouth of Anchises. The superiority of some foreign nations, and especially of the Greeks, in the lazy arts of peace, would be admitted with disdainful candor; but preëminence in all the qualities which fit a people to subdue and govern mankind would be claimed for the Romans.

The following lay belongs to the latest age of Latin ballad-poetry Nævis and Livius Andronicus were probably among the children whose mothers held them up to see the chariot of Curius go by. The minstrel who sang on that day might possibly have lived to read the first hexameters of Ennius, and to see the first comedies of Plautus. His poem, as might be expected, shows a much wider acquaintance with the geography, manners, and productions of remote nations, than would have been found in compositions of the age of Camillus But he troubles himself little about dates, and having heard travellers talk with admiration of the Colossus of Rhodes, and of the structures and gardens with which the Macedonian king of Syria had embellished their residence on the banks of the Orontes, he has never thought of inquiring whether these things existed in the age of Romulus.

The Prophecy of Capys

A Lay Sung at the Banquet in the Capitol, on the Day Whereon Manius Curius Dentatus, a Second Time Consul, Triumphed Over King
Pyrrhus and the Tarentines, in the Year of the City CCCCLXXIX.

I

Now slain is King Amulius,
Of the great Sylvian line,
Who reigned in Alba Longa,
On the throne of Aventine.
Slain is the Ponfiff Camers,
Who spake the words of doom:
"The children to the Tiber,
The mother to the tomb."

II

In Alba's lake no fisher

His net to-day is flinging;
  On the dark rind of Alba's oaks
    To-day no axe is ringing;
  The yoke hangs o'er the manger;
    The scythe lies in the hay:
  Through all the Alban villages
    No work is done to-day.

III

And every Alban burgher
  Hath donned his whitest gown;
And every head in Alba
  Weareth a poplar crown;
And every Alban door-post
  With boughs and flowers is gay,
For to-day the dead are living,
  The lost are found to-day.

IV

They were doomed by a bloody king,
  They were doomed by a lying priest,
They were cast on the raging flood,
  They were tracked by the raging beast;
Raging beast and raging flood
  Alike have spared the prey;
And to-day the dead are living,
  The lost are found to-day.

V

The troubled river knew them,
  And smoothed his yellow foam,
And gently rocked the cradle
  That bore the fate of Rome.
The ravening she-wolf knew them,
  And licked them o'er and o'er,
And gave them of her own fierce milk,
  Rich with raw flesh and gore.
Twenty winters, twenty springs,
  Since then have rolled away;
And to-day the dead are living:
  The lost are found to-day.

VI

Blithe it was to see the twins,

Right goodly youths and tall,
Marching from Alba Longa
  To their old grandsire's hall.
Along their path fresh garlands
  Are hung from tree to tree:
Before them stride the pipers,
  Piping a note of glee.

VII

On the right goes Romulus,
  With arms to the elbows red,
And in his hand a broadsword,
  And on the blade a head—
A head in an iron helmet,
  With horse-hair hanging down,
A shaggy head, a swarthy head,
  Fixed in a ghastly frown—
The head of King Amulius
  Of the great Sylvian line,
Who reigned in Alba Longa,
  On the throne of Aventine.

VIII

On the left side goes Remus,
  With wrists and fingers red,
And in his hand a boar-spear,
  And on the point a head—
A wrinkled head and aged,
  With silver beard and hair,
And holy fillets round it,
  Such as the pontiffs wear—
The head of ancient Camers,
  Who spake the words of doom:
"The children to the Tiber;
  The mother to the tomb."

IX

Two and two behind the twins
  Their trusty comrades go,
Four and forty valiant men,
  With club, and axe, and bow.
On each side every hamlet
  Pours forth its joyous crowd,
Shouting lads and baying dogs,
  And children laughing loud,

And old men weeping fondly
    As Rhea's boys go by,
And maids who shriek to see the heads,
    Yet, shrieking, press more nigh.

X

So marched they along the lake;
    They marched by fold and stall,
By cornfield and by vineyard,
    Unto the old man's hall.

XI

In the hall-gate sat Capys,
    Capys, the sightless seer;
From head to foot he trembled
    As Romulus drew near.
And up stood stiff his thin white hair,
    And his blind eyes flashed fire:
"Hail! foster child of the wondrous nurse!
    Hail! son of the wondrous sire!"

XII

"But thou—what dost thou here
    In the old man's peaceful hall?
What doth the eagle in the coop,
    The bison in the stall?
Our corn fills many a garner;
    Our vines clasp many a tree;
Our flocks are white on many a hill:
    But these are not for thee.

XIII

"For thee no treasure ripens
    In the Tartessian mine;
For thee no ship brings precious bales
    Across the Libyan brine;
Thou shalt not drink from amber;
    Thou shalt not rest on down;
Arabia shall not steep thy locks,
    Nor Sidon tinge thy gown.

XIV

"Leave gold and myrrh and jewels,

Rich table and soft bed,
To them who of man's seed are born,
    Whom woman's milk have fed.
Thou wast not made for lucre,
    For pleasure, nor for rest;
Thou, that art sprung from the War-god's loins,
    And hast tugged at the she-wolf's breast.

XV

"From sunrise unto sunset
    All earth shall hear thy fame:
A glorious city thou shalt build,
    And name it by thy name:
And there, unquenched through ages,
    Like Vesta's sacred fire,
Shall live the spirit of thy nurse,
    The spirit of thy sire.

XVI

"The ox toils through the furrow,
    Obedient to the goad;
The patient ass, up flinty paths,
    Plods with his weary load:
With whine and bound the spaniel
    His master's whistle hears;
And the sheep yields her patiently
    To the loud-clashing shears.

XVII

"But thy nurse will hear no master,
    Thy nurse will bear no load;
And woe to them that shear her,
    And woe to them that goad!
When all the pack, loud baying,
    Her bloody lair surrounds,
She dies in silence, biting hard,
    Amidst the dying hounds.

XVIII

"Pomona loves the orchard;
    And Liber loves the vine;
And Pales loves the straw-built shed
    Warm with the breath of kine;
And Venus loves the whispers

Of plighted youth and maid,
In April's ivory moonlight
    Beneath the chestnut shade.

XIX

"But thy father loves the clashing
    Of broadsword and of shield:
He loves to drink the steam that reeks
    From the fresh battlefield:
He smiles a smile more dreadful
    Than his own dreadful frown,
When he sees the thick black cloud of smoke
    Go up from the conquered town.

XX

"And such as is the War-god,
    The author of thy line,
And such as she who suckled thee,
    Even such be thou and thine.
Leave to the soft Campanian
    His baths and his perfumes;
Leave to the sordid race of Tyre
    Their dyeing-vats and looms;
Leave to the sons of Carthage
    The rudder and the oar;
Leave to the Greek his marble Nymphs
    And scrolls of wordy lore.

XXI

"Thine, Roman, is the pilum:
    Roman, the sword is thine,
The even trench, the bristling mound,
    The legion's ordered line;
And thine the wheels of triumph,
    Which with their laurelled train
Move slowly up the shouting streets
    To Jove's eternal flame.

XXII

"Beneath thy yoke the Volscian
    Shall vail his lofty brow;
Soft Capua's curled revellers
    Before thy chairs shall bow:
The Lucumoes of Arnus

Shall quake thy rods to see;
And the proud Samnite's heart of steel
    Shall yield to only thee.

XXIII

"The Gaul shall come against thee
    From the land of snow and night;
Thou shalt give his fair-haired armies
    To the raven and the kite.

XXIV

"The Greek shall come against thee,
    The conqueror of the East.
Beside him stalks to battle
    The huge earth-shaking beast,
The beast on whom the castle
    With all its guards doth stand,
The beast who hath between his eyes
    The serpent for a hand.
First march the bold Epirotes,
    Wedged close with shield and spear
And the ranks of false Tarentum
    Are glittering in the rear.

XXV

"The ranks of false Tarentum
    Like hunted sheep shall fly:
In vain the bold Epirotes
    Shall round their standards die:
And Apennine's gray vultures
    Shall have a noble feast
On the fat and the eyes
    Of the the huge earth-shaking beast.

XXVI

"Hurrah! for the good weapons
    That keep the War-god's land.
Hurrah! for Rome's stout pilum
    In a stout Roman hand.
Hurrah! for Rome's short broadsword
    That through the thick array
Of levelled spears and serried shields
    Hews deep its gory way.

XXVII

"Hurrah! for the great triumph
    That stretches many a mile.
Hurrah! for the wan captives
    That pass in endless file.
Ho! bold Epirotes, whither
    Hath the Red King taken flight?
Ho! dogs of false Tarentum,
    Is not the gown washed white?

XXVIII

"Hurrah! for the great triumph
    That stretches many a mile.
Hurrah! for the rich dye of Tyre,
    And the fine web of Nile,
The helmets gay with plumage
    Torn from the pheasant's wings,
The belts set thick with starry gem
    That shone on Indian kings,
The urns of massy silver,
    The goblets rough with gold,
The many-colored tablets bright
    With loves and wars of old,
The stone that breathes and struggles,
    The brass that seems to speak;—
Such cunning they who dwell on high
    Have given unto the Greek.

XXIX

"Hurrah! for Manius Curius,
    The bravest son of Rome,
Thrice in utmost need sent forth,
    Thrice drawn in triumph home.
Weave, weave, for Manius Curius
    The third embroidered gown:
Make ready the third lofty car,
    And twine the third green crown;
And yoke the steeds of Rosea
    With necks like a bended bow,
And deck the bull, Mevania's bull,
    The bull as white as snow.

XXX

"Blest and thrice blest the Roman

Who sees Rome's brightest day,
Who sees that long victorious pomp
    Wind down the Sacred Way,
And through the bellowing Forum,
    And round the Suppliant's Grove,
Up to the everlasting gates
    Of Capitolian Jove.

XXXI

"Then where, o'er two bright havens,
    The towers of Corinth frown;
Where the gigantic King of Day
    On his own Rhodes looks down;
Where oft Orontes murmurs
    Beneath the laurel shades;
Where Nile reflects the endless length
    Of dark red colonnades;
Where in the still deep water,
    Sheltered from waves and blasts,
Bristles the dusky forest
    Of Byrsa's thousand masts;
Where fur-clad hunters wander
    Amidst the northern ice;
Where through the sand of morning-land
    The camel bears the spice;
Where Atlas flings his shadow
    Far o'er the western foam,
Shall be great fear on all who hear
    The might name of Rome."

THE END

INTRODUCTION

The nineteenth century was a fascinating and vital formative period in Western literature since it provided the fundamental backdrop for the formation and emergence of contemporary literary traditions and styles as we know them today.

The Victorian Period, named after Queen Victoria's reign from 1837 to 1901, was characterised by significant cultural and creative triumphs, social and technological developments, and significant political and economic transformation. It was a time of development and expansion for Britain, as it became the world's largest empire; it was also a time of significant social and cultural transformation in America. Rapid industrialisation and urbanisation resulted in a lively literary environment with a diverse spectrum of genres and styles. Popular literary genres at the time included sentimental novels, gothic novels, and regionalist writing. Additional research, for example, shows that the Romantic, Symbolist, and Realist movements, as well as a variety of social and economic circumstances that dominated the twentieth century, all had their origins and predecessors in the nineteenth century.

MOVEMENTS AND LITERATURE

ROMANTICISM

Romanticism, with its stress on sensation and the irrational, emerged in the nineteenth century as a significant literary and cultural movement. The 18th century, on the other hand, was regarded to be the age of intelligence, reasoning, and the mind. Romanticism, which emerged from the late-nineteenth-century German Sturm und Drang ("Stress and Storm") movement and whose notable members included Goethe and Friedrich Schiller, was marked by a focus on the individual, subjective, mystical, emotional, and inner life.

Writers and poets such as William Wordsworth, Samuel Taylor Coleridge, and John Keats in England, and Johann Wolfgang von Goethe and Friedrich Schiller in Germany, sought to capture the sublime in nature and the depth of human emotion in their works.

The Romantic movement was also marked by a fascination with the past, the mystical, and the exotic. This was evident in the rise of Gothic literature, with novels such as Mary Shelley's 'Frankenstein' (1818) and the poems of Edgar Allan Poe. Romanticism was not just a literary movement; it also had profound impacts on art and music, inspiring artists like J.M.W. Turner and composers like Ludwig van Beethoven. Ultimately, Romanticism represented a fundamental shift in cultural attitudes, offering a new perspective on the nature of creativity, the purpose of art, and the role of the artist in society.

- *Rousseau*

Jean-Jacques Rousseau was a towering intellectual figure whose ideas shaped the 19th century, despite his death in 1778. His writings profoundly influenced both the Age of Enlightenment and the Romantic movements, creating a bridge between these two key periods. Rousseau challenged the primacy of reason advocated by his Enlightenment contemporaries, arguing that feelings and emotions were also essential in understanding the human experience. His novel, "Julie, or the New Heloise" (1761), is considered a precursor to Romanticism, emphasizing passion and sentiment.

- *Early Romantic poets*

The late 18th and early 19th century Romantic English poets William Wordsworth and Samuel Taylor Coleridge, who released their collection of poems Lyrical Ballads in 1798, are considered the forefathers of this style. As seen by the works of Pushkin in Russia, Ugo Foscolo and Giacomo Leopardi in Italy, José de Espronceda in Spain, and Giacomo Leopardi, the Romantic poetry movement was popular and flourished throughout Europe and beyond.

- *American Romanticism*

American Romanticism, a movement that spanned the mid-19th century, was a reaction against the rationalism of the Age of Enlightenment and a manifestation of the ethos of individualism that was central to the American frontier spirit. It encapsulated a broad range of human experience and played out differently across various genres, exploring themes like the supernatural, the power of nature, and the potential of the individual.

James Fenimore Cooper's historical adventure novels, such as "The Last of the Mohicans" (1826), created a uniquely American kind of Romantic hero - the rugged, self-reliant frontiersman. Edgar Allan Poe took a darker route, delving into the eerie and supernatural in tales like "The Fall of the House of Usher" (1839) and "The Raven" (1845). These works were representative of the Gothic element within Romanticism, exploring the darker recesses of the human psyche.

Walt Whitman, with his groundbreaking collection "Leaves of Grass" (1855), embodied another aspect of American Romanticism. His free verse celebrated the individual, democratic values, and the spiritual significance of everyday life.

Finally, the Transcendentalist movement, led by Ralph Waldo Emerson and Henry David Thoreau, elevated the individual conscience above societal norms. Emerson's essay "Self-Reliance" (1841) became a key text, while Thoreau's "Walden" (1854) documented his experiment in simple living and immersion in nature.

Together, these authors and works shaped the American Romantic movement, offering new perspectives on the human experience and inspiring readers to break free from societal constraints and explore their own individual paths.

- *Second Generation Romantic poets*

To discover the "truth" of things, the Romantics went to people's emotions, which were grounded in and exemplified by interaction with nature and the primordial self, rather than logical inquiry. Second-generation Romantic writers John Keats, Lord Byron, and Percy Bysshe Shelley's writings are good examples of these points of view.

POST ROMANTICISM

- *Parnassianism*

The works of French poets Théophile Gautier and Charles Baudelaire are examples of Parnassianism, which can be considered as an extension of early Romantic viewpoints with its emphasis on aesthetics and the concept of art for the sake of art. Schopenhauer's philosophical ideas had an impact as well. Devotees attempted to address their foreign and old subjects of fascination in a more controlled, formal manner, retreating from the excess passion and sentimentality of the Romantic movement.

- *Impressionism and Symbolism*

Claude Monet and other Paris-based painters contributed to the development of impressionism, which first arose in painting and then in music in France near the end of the nineteenth century. Impressionism was a painting style that attempted to reflect the visual world as accurately as possible by employing the shifting qualities of light and colour as seen via human perception and experience.

Symbolism is characterised as a departure from naturalism and realism in favour of a harsher, more truthful portrayal of the world, with a concentration on the ordinary rather than the extraordinary. Symbolist poets, such as Gustave Kahn and Ezra Pound, employed imagery to "evoke" rather than portray or describe.

THE GOTHIC NOVEL

The Gothic Novel, a vibrant subgenre of Romantic fiction, emerged in Europe towards the end of the 18th century. Pioneers in this field include Horace Walpole with his ground-breaking novel "The Castle of Otranto" (1765), and Ann Radcliffe, whose work "The Mysteries of Udolpho" elevated the genre. The term 'Gothic' is derived from Gothic architecture, a common setting in these novels, characterized by crumbling castles, haunted monasteries, and dark forests, which lent an eerie atmosphere to the narratives.

Distinct from typical supernatural tales, Gothic novels often dealt with themes of ancestral curses and past sins haunting the present, exploring the darker recesses of the human psyche and the effects of terror and horror on it. This was further explored in the 19th-century through seminal works such as Mary Shelley's "Frankenstein" (1818), Sir Walter Scott's "Bride of Lammermoor" (1819), E.T.A.

Hoffmann's "The Devil's Elixirs" (1815), Emily Bronte's "Wuthering Heights" (1847), Robert Louis Stevenson's "The Strange Case of Dr. Jekyll and Mr. Hyde" (1886), and Bram Stoker's "Dracula" (1897).

Even beyond these iconic pieces, the influence of the Gothic novel can be seen in many well-regarded Victorian works. Charles Dickens' "Bleak House" (1852-1853) and "Great Expectations" (1861), for example, both incorporate elements of the Gothic tradition, reflecting its broad impact on the literature of the time. This genre, with its exploration of the sublime, the uncanny, and the spectral, significantly contributed to the richness and depth of 19th-century literature.

POPULAR PHILOSOPHY

- *German Idealism*

German Idealism, a significant philosophical movement of the late 18th and early 19th centuries, was pioneered by figures such as Johann Gottlieb Fichte. Building upon the metaphysical insights of Immanuel Kant, Fichte proposed a dynamic conception of the self as a constantly evolving entity. Georg Wilhelm Friedrich Hegel further extended this idea by emphasizing the importance of historical and dialectical thinking in understanding the self. In contrast, Arthur Schopenhauer diverged from Hegel's path and argued for a return to Kant's transcendental philosophy.

- *Marxism*

The philosophical and political ideology known as Marxism was born out of the intellectual partnership of Karl Marx and Friedrich Engels. Their seminal work, "The Communist Manifesto" (1848), presented a critique of capitalism, asserting its inherent instability and predicting its eventual replacement by socialist and, subsequently, communist systems. This work laid the foundation for the later international communist movement.

- *Positivism*

The philosophical position of Positivism was proposed by August Comte, advocating the belief that genuine knowledge is inherently empirical and verifiable. Comte argued that such knowledge derives from observable phenomena and subsequent logical and mathematical reasoning, excluding innate knowledge or metaphysical speculation

- *Social Darwinism*

The concept of Social Darwinism sought to apply the biological principles of natural selection and survival of the fittest, as outlined in Charles Darwin's "On the Origin of Species", to societal and political contexts. Proponents included Francis Galton, who maintained that cognitive abilities were as heritable as physical characteristics, and advocated for societal intervention in reproductive practices to prevent the over-breeding of "less fit" individuals. Similarly, Herbert Spencer, in his work "The Social Organism" (1860), likened society to a living organism, evolving and adapting according to Darwinian principles.

SOCIAL, ECONOMIC AND POLITICAL IMPACTS

- *The Industrial Revolution*

The Industrial Revolution, which took place between the late 18th and a time between 1820 and 1840, was a time of great social, political, and economic uprisings and change that involved the challenging transition from largely manual production methods to mechanical manufacturing methods, particularly in the fields of textiles, steam power, iron making, and the invention of machine tools. Agriculture had previously been the foundation of the European economy, and it was also a time when basic political, scientific, and religious ideas were unravelled to their core.

As a result of this mechanisation, a considerable number of people were transported from rural villages to metropolitan regions, resulting in a significant increase in population and the establishment of new, larger cities. The advancement of new technology resulted in the establishment of factories, a dehumanising and horrifying method of labour, particularly child labour, and a capitalist way of life. Because cities were unable to accommodate the rapidly rising population, there were overcrowded slums and terribly deplorable living conditions, as described in books such as Friedrich Engels' The Condition of the Working Class in England, published in 1844.

Elizabeth Barrett Browning's The Cry of the Children, Thomas Hardy's Tess of the D'Urbervilles, and works by author and philosopher Thomas Carlyle warned of the threat to society posed by these inhumane conditions and the profit-focused, materialistic ideals of what Dickens referred to as the "mechanical age" in his novels Hard Times and Oliver Twist.

- *Slavery and the Abolionist movement*

The 19th century in the United States was a time of great political upheaval and moral conflict. At the heart of these struggles was the question of slavery - the practice of owning human beings as property and forcing them to labor for the benefit of their owners. Slavery was deeply entrenched in the southern states, where it was seen as essential to the region's economy and way of life. But in the north, a growing abolitionist movement called for the immediate and unconditional end of slavery, seeing it as a fundamental violation of human rights and a stain on the nation's conscience.

These debates over slavery were not just academic or theoretical - they were deeply intertwined with the politics and culture of the time. The question of whether or not to allow slavery in new territories was a key issue in the lead-up to the Civil War, which ultimately erupted in 1861 and tore the nation apart. But even before the war, tensions over slavery were high, and political leaders grappled with how to address this thorny and divisive issue.

While the United States grappled with the practice and morality of slavery within its own borders, across the Atlantic, the United Kingdom was undergoing its own transformation in the 19th century regarding slavery. In 1807, the UK took a decisive step with the passage of the Slave Trade Act, which outlawed the transatlantic slave trade. This was followed by the Slavery Abolition Act of 1833, effectively ending slavery throughout the British Empire, except for areas under the administration of the East India Company, and in the territories of Ceylon (now Sri Lanka) and Saint Helena. This Act marked a critical turning point in the global fight against slavery.

This momentous development was not without its influences. Several influential works published during this period galvanized public opinion and shaped the discourse on slavery and abolition. Thomas Clarkson's 'An Essay on the Slavery and Commerce of the Human Species' (1786) offered a thorough critique of slavery, leading to its expanded edition in 1808. Another influential work, 'The History of Mary Prince' (1831), was the first account of a black woman's life published in the UK, detailing her experiences as an enslaved person in Bermuda, which sparked public interest and became a tool in the hands of abolitionists.

In tandem, anti-slavery sentiment was reflected in the literary world as well. For instance, Elizabeth Barrett Browning's influential poem, 'The Runaway Slave at Pilgrim's Point' (1847), powerfully condemned the institution of slavery.

- *The Rise of Nationalism and Imperialism*

The 19th century marked a pivotal period in global history, as it saw the rise of two influential ideologies: Nationalism and Imperialism. Both had profound implications for the world, reshaping political, economic, and social landscapes.

Nationalism emerged as a potent political force, rooted in the belief that individuals sharing a common language, culture, or ancestry constituted a nation. This ideology played a critical role in the unification of fragmented regions into cohesive nation-states. The unification of Italy in 1861 and Germany in 1871 stand as two of the most significant examples of nationalism's impact. Both unifications were driven by charismatic leaders— Camilo di Cavour in Italy and Otto von Bismarck in Germany— and the shared desire of the people to form a unified national identity. The emergence of nationalism also led to a rise in independence movements in various parts of the world, leading to the downfall of old empires and the birth of new nations.

Imperialism, on the other hand, was driven by the ambitions of the powerful Western nations to expand their influence and control over other parts of the globe. Rooted in a belief in cultural and racial superiority, as well as economic motivations, imperialism led to the colonization of large parts of Africa, Asia, and the Pacific. Key events during this period include the scramble for Africa (1881-1914), where European powers divided the continent among themselves, and the Opium Wars (1839-1860), which marked the beginning of Western imperial control over China.

The expansion of the British Empire, which, at its height, was the largest empire in history, is another prominent example of 19th-century imperialism. This period also witnessed the rise of the United States as an imperial power, with its acquisition of territories in the Caribbean and Pacific, notably following the Spanish-American War in 1898.

Both nationalism and imperialism had profound and lasting impacts on global politics, economics, and societies, the effects of which continue to be felt into the present day. They shaped national identities, redrawed the world map, and sowed the seeds for many of the conflicts and power dynamics of the 20th century.

-      *Science and influential Non-Fiction works*

Throughout the nineteenth century, Victorians' drive to understand and categorise the natural world played an important part in the development of scientific theory and understanding. Charles Darwin's works, such as the well-known On the Origin of Species (1859), would have a dramatic and far-reaching impact due to their innovative idea of evolution, which contradicted many of the time's established notions and religious beliefs.

The French Revolution: A History, published in 1837, and On Heroes, Hero-Worship, and the Heroic in History, published in 1841, are two other important non-fiction works from the period that influenced political thinking in the mid-nineteenth century.

KEY HISTORICAL EVENTS

- ## *The Acts of Union and Treaty of Amiens*

Following the French Revolution and the Irish Rebellion in the late 18th century, which brought unpredictability and instability, the Acts of Union were passed in 1800, combining Britain and Ireland to form the United Kingdom.

The Treaty of Amiens brought the Second Coalition French Revolutionary War to a close, as well as the disputes between France and the United Kingdom. The effect, however, was fleeting, since the Napoleonic Wars began in just three years.

- ## *US expansion*

With their newly gained independence, the United States chose to purchase the Louisiana Purchase in 1803 in order to double their size and expand their control over the Mississippi River. Native Americans occupy a substantial portion of the region, which was purchased for $15 million from the French First Republic.

- ## *Napoleonic Wars*

Napoleon decimated the Russian and Austrian troops in 1805, but his plans to invade England were thwarted when Admiral Nelson soundly defeated the French and Spanish armies at the Battle of Trafalgar, cementing the nation's dominance over the oceans.

During the Russian invasion, the French army suffered tremendous losses— up to 380,000 soldiers died— and Napoleon's previous image as an unbeatable general was shattered. The French king abdicated and was exiled to Elba following his loss in the War of the Sixth Coalition in 1814.

- ## *British and Russian empire expansion*

Following France's loss, Britain and Russia rose to prominence as the world's two largest powers, with Russia expanding its sphere of influence to include Central Asia and the Caucasus and Britain increasing its foreign possessions to include Canada, Australia, South Africa, and Africa. The British East India Company was dissolved as a result of the Indian Rebellion of 1857, which was a widespread insurrection against colonial rule. Later, the British Crown assumed direct administration and founded the British Raj.

- *Opium wars*

By the mid-nineteenth century, China experienced severe opium problems as a result of the opening of trade with the West and the illicit trafficking in the drug coordinated by British entrepreneurs seeking to earn money at the trading ports. On the basis of free trade principles, Britain resisted the emperor's attempt to outlaw its sale, resulting in the First Opium War and the Treaty of Nanking in 1842, which permitted the drug trade to continue while handing over control of Hong Kong to the British.

The Taiping Rebellion of 1856 set the stage for the second Opium War, in which France and Britain collaborated. The 1860 Peking Convention, which legalised the opium trade and forced the surrender of additional provinces, resulted in the early nineteenth-century demise of the Qing dynasty.

- *The 1848 Revolutions*

The 1848 Revolutions, also known as the Springtime of the Nations, were a series of political upheavals that occurred in Europe and the rest of the world in 1848. The main purpose of these uprisings was to abolish previous monarchical authority and establish free nation governments.

Nationalists in Italy organised revolutions in Sicily and the Italian peninsula republics in order to construct a liberal government and break free from Austrian domination. The February Revolution in France occurred in Paris following the crackdown on the campagne des banquets, a violent insurgency against the monarchy that resulted in King Louis Philippe's overthrow. Germany, Denmark, Hungary, Galicia, Sweden, and Switzerland were among the other countries that revolted against the Habsburg Monarchy.

- *Abolitionism and the end of slavery*

The Atlantic slave trade was outlawed in the United States in 1808, and slavery was outlawed throughout the British Empire by the Slavery Abolition Act of 1833. Abolitionism triumphed in the nineteenth century. Abolitionism persisted in the United States until the Civil War ended in 1865, when the Thirteenth Amendment to the Constitution was ratified, officially abolishing slavery in the country.

- *Women's Suffrage movement*

"The call for women's suffrage, the right for women to vote, gained momentum in the 19th century. The cause was propelled by landmark events such as the Seneca Falls Convention in 1848, often considered the birthplace of the American women's rights movement, and the first National Women's Rights Convention in 1850. Key feminist literary works, such as Margaret Fuller's 'Woman in the Nineteenth Century' (1845), which advocated for women's independence and equality, and Sarah Grimké's 'The Equality of the Sexes and the Condition of Women' (1838), helped shape the discourse surrounding women's rights.

In spite of initial failures to secure voting rights during the 1870s, suffragists pressed forward with relentless determination, advocating state-by-state for a constitutional amendment to enfranchise women. The U.S. state of Wyoming led the way in 1869, becoming the first state to grant women the right to vote in all elections.

Across the Atlantic, the UK suffragette movement found a dynamic leader in Emmeline Pankhurst. Pankhurst, who became involved in the suffrage movement in the 1880s, was instrumental in shifting the strategy of the movement towards direct action and civil disobedience, a strategy that would ultimately lead to women achieving the right to vote in 1918 for women over 30 and in 1928 for all women over 21, leveling the voting age with men."

Made in the USA
Middletown, DE
11 November 2024

64361505R00061